The People Management Formula

The People Management Formula

Six Indispensable Human Relations Practices Used by Bosses Everyone Admires Most

Part of the *S.O.L.I.D.* *People Management Series*
*Skills for Organizational Leadership and Individual Development

Stephen E. Kohn and Vincent D. O'Connell

Writer's Showcase
New York   Lincoln   Shanghai

The People Management Formula
Six Indispensable Human Relations Practices
Used by Bosses Everyone Admires Most

Writer's Showcase
an imprint of iUniverse, Inc.

For information address:
iUniverse
2021 Pine Lake Road, Suite 100
Lincoln, NE 68512
www.iuniverse.com

ISBN: 0-595-24498-X

Printed in the United States of America

To our families, who teach us every day about inspiration, loyalty, performance and the value of human relationships in a meaningful life.

Contents

Foreword

For many years, our work has been focused on resolving "people prob-lems" that occur at the workplace. Each consulting assignment has its own special aspects and challenges, often related to the client firm's industry, size, executive management style and organizational struc-ture. But over the course of time that we have spent helping many com-panies solve seemingly unique management human relations problems, we have observed a pattern to the interventions we plan and imple-ment. The characters and situations change a bit, but the management skills we tend to focus on are essentially the same. It finally struck us that our practice centered on a *model*, a formula applicable in nearly all circumstances. Almost invariably, a core set of management human relations practices served as a starting point for developing our clients' leadership skills.

Often, as aspects of this model crystallized either during formal, "peer review"-type assessments of our respective caseloads or just during conversations over morning coffee, one of us would announce playfully, "Now, <u>that</u> will be a chapter in our book." Of course, up until this point, writing the book has always been, let's say, "in the conceptual stage"—a future goal we hoped to accomplish for ourselves and for our consult-ing firm. Eventually, we realized that we needed to practice what we preach. Many times, we have exhorted our client managers to stop pro-crastinating and to move forward productively with a prudent idea or personal goal. So, part of our impetus in completing our book was sim-ply avoiding guilt. How ashamed would we would feel when con-fronting clients about their goal-delaying tactics, when we too were all talk and no action? It was time to roll up our sleeves and get the book done!

The other driver behind completing the book had a more positive, fulfilling tone. We had a real interest in sharing our model with a broader business audience. We believed in our work, and we wanted to describe it to those beyond our own clientele.

Once we began to take this book project seriously, we realized that we needed a plan. We decided that a book project should be designed like many other projects that professionals assume in day-to-day business management. We agreed that documenting a core purpose and identifying a target audience would be great places to start. *"Clarifying a Mission"* and *"Knowing the Customer"* are transcendent values that apply to any process aimed at producing high quality work, regardless of what the product or service might be. We believed that producing a book on leadership skills should be no exception.

Consequently, the first questions we posed to each other were: Why are we undertaking this effort? What are we trying to accomplish? To deliver quality, our answer needed to be more than a perfunctory, intellectual exercise. We needed to *own* the purpose behind the book, knowing that we would refer back to it often.

We conceived our mission as follows:

> *This book shares our approach to developing leaders' human relations skills, so that managers who implement our model become more productive in their positions, create advancement opportunities for themselves in their careers and apply these skills to a broad range of interpersonal situations in their own lives.*

In considering how to best achieve this mission, we felt our next task was to assess, "Who will be interested in the material we intend to share?" We needed to identify some basic assumptions that hold true about our book's prospective audience. In essence, we needed to confirm to ourselves just <u>who our customers are</u>.

Some macro-level, "big picture" assumptions about our potential customers would be helpful to generate. Our book is about leadership "people skills," so it makes sense that our readers would bring a strong appreciation for the more interpersonal aspects of professional management. We expect that this appreciation for human relations skills is driven either by experience or by seasoned observation. In order to have experience or seasoned perspectives, individuals who comprise our book's audience are likely either to hold leadership positions at work or foresee themselves having supervisory responsibilities in the near future.

Further, our readers are no doubt intrigued by the disparity in management performance that exists among different supervisors. Most of us have been exposed, either directly or indirectly, to strong managers as well as to those who are woefully deficient in basic human relations competencies. Our readers are likely to ask themselves, "Why do people want to work hard for one manager and want to quit on or avoid interactions with another?" Further, our readers have seen how workplace conflicts distract an organization from optimal productivity. One natural objective for anyone reading this book will be to learn ways of avoiding such discord and animosity to the greatest extent possible.

We expect that most of our potential readers have been exposed on some level to previous training about supervisory human relations skills. This training might have been sponsored by one's employer, by institutions that provide academic preparation for management responsibilities or by professional continuing education courses. We assume our readers are likely to have a basic familiarity with many of the "do's" and "don't's" of leading other people from a human relations perspective. However, we also expect that our readers have an interest in gaining a greater understanding about broader behavioral science subjects, such as social psychology, organizational dynamics, motivational theory, personality type and individual psychological development.

Indeed, learning about leadership people skills is likely to be part "vocation" and part "avocation" for our readers. Many of you have addressed—or are in the process of addressing—ways to upgrade your interpersonal skills through very individualized self-improvement activities such as mentoring, coaching or even counseling/psychotherapy. As we will emphasize later, self-awareness is crucial to leadership success.

We have come to the conclusion that there are several essential human relations skills that need to be mastered in order for individuals to show improvement in the way they:

- lead others in an organization, and;
- grow as individuals.

Again, this is aligned with our book's mission. We believe that the former (skill set related to organizational leadership) is integrally connected to and, in fact, potentiates the latter (skills that foster individual development outside work).

Our challenge in writing this book was twofold: first, we needed to organize and "make the case" for a sensible, pertinent model highlighting these essential people management skills; secondly, we needed to document the exercises we use and the debriefing questions we ask after the exercises are completed that help develop these people management skills in our clients. We intend for the book to be part content—descriptions and clarifications about the model itself—and part "process manual," or a description of ways to develop skills by putting them into practice.

Hopefully, the mission we drafted ties in well with your personal and professional interests. We also hope that we have made the correct assumptions about readers who will be interested in the material we are presenting. One way for us to know is by receiving feedback from you.

We would love to hear your thoughts, opinions, clarifications, experiences or ideas about what you have read and its application to your work. This feedback process helps us complete the project management "loop" that began with our attempts to identify the book's mission and understand our customer base. Also, it keeps the project alive. It is exciting to gain fresh and dynamic insights about one's work over a more extended period of time.

It may help you as well. Assembling and sharing your reactions to some of the human relations challenges you face may raise your awareness of specific issues that hold particular importance to you. We hope you take advantage of this offer to initiate a dialogue with us.

Here is our contact information.

> *Work & People Solutions*
> *701 Westchester Ave., Suite 308W*
> *White Plains, NY 10604*
> *914-686-2552 or online at:*
> *bookcomments@workandpeople.com*

You will notice we have established a unique email address for your feed-back. Send your messages to us at _bookcomments@workandpeople.com_. We promise to respond to your input. Thanks in advance to those of you who take the effort to provide it. We sincerely appreciate it.

Introduction

Can you think of the direct supervisor for whom you most enjoyed working? Most of us have had a supervisor that we respected. Perhaps you have one currently. In either case, this individual is a person with a special set of management qualities that inspired or inspires you. No doubt, he or she made your job easier, more fulfilling and more enjoyable.

But just what are the qualities of the prototypical "favorite boss?" Asked another way—from a management development perspective—what skills need to be developed so that one can become the boss that people admire most?

We are going to try to answer this question for managers. In the course of organizing our thoughts about how to do so, we paid close attention to <u>three premises</u> that we are always very mindful of when we engage in human resources development activities for client organizations.

1. <u>*People skills are integral to effective management.*</u> *People skills matter to managers at all levels of an organization.* They matter in an innumerable amount of ways. They matter in terms of improving workplace productivity. They matter in terms of how well one succeeds in pursuing a career path of increased authority and responsibility. They matter in terms of minimizing incidences of time-consuming and distracting conflicts with subordinates.

The fact is that successful organizations prioritize human relations skills in their management culture. Organizations that people want to work for understand that people management skills galvanize employees' morale, loyalty and work performance. Consider the graph shown below that is commonly used to describe the varying imperatives of applied management skills as one assumes more supervisory responsibilities:

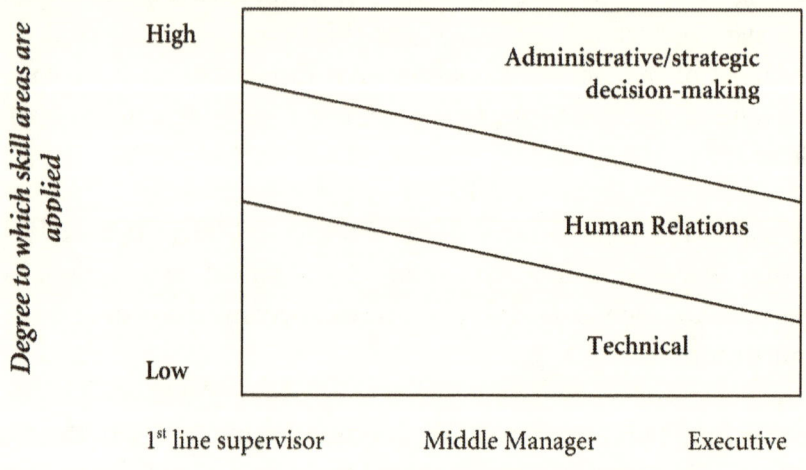

Degree of Management Authority

The graph demonstrates how the percentage of a manager's job that involves more administrative and strategic decision-making skills increases with the level of senior executive status one attains within an organization. But no matter what level of responsibility a manager has within the organization, the need to apply human relations skills remains both significant and consistent. From the front line supervisor through top executive ranks, a dedication to effective human relations practices is essential to the performance of managers' roles. For productivity and performance to be max-imized system-wide within an organization, all supervisors need to apply consistent and refined human relations skills within their leadership function.

If people skills matter to managers, if they are highly salient to organizational success, then it is logical that progressive managers will want to understand these skills more and find ways to develop them. Within any profession, it is important to maintain a focus on "best practices." We believe our model, developed through extensive research and actual experience, synthesizes the best available practices in an essential aspect of management practice: human relations skills.

2. ***People skills can be learned and developed.*** People are capable of real, positive change. People grow. They <u>can</u> learn new, more productive ways of interacting with others, both in personal and business contexts. Certainly, these skills come more naturally for some than they do for others. But everyone has the ability to show improvement in human relations competencies. Honestly, we have yet to work with any client who never had human relations competencies and never will.

3. ***Managers are very busy, and training must be efficient and relevant.*** We know that you are busy with a range of business priorities. We expect that you are going to be best served by brief, understandable training models. We believe that *the more straightforward and concise the content, recommendations and exercises we present, the better.* We expect that if we met face-to-face in a real coaching session, you would be likely to say, "Keep it simple for me, and I'll follow the program. Make it confusing, overly complicated or very time-consuming and I'm likely to revert back to the way I am accustomed to interacting with others."

Most managers prefer highly readable, concise summaries of the topic at hand. They prefer training that is time-efficient and well-organized. We believe our model meets a high standard for relevance and for rapid comprehension of its essential principles.

The full range of management human relations skills can be pretty overwhelming. Our model is purposefully confined to just six practices that every manager can build into their professional management repertoire in a time-efficient manner. Ideally, the skills we describe will relate quite directly and rapidly to interactions you have with the people under your supervision. Our objective is to "keep it simple," but targeted and useful.

1

Management Human Relations: The <u>Real</u> "People Strategy"

Organizations are focusing on "people strategies"

These days, it is very popular for organizations to formulate a "people strategy." This strategy documents a concerted effort to leverage human capital in attaining the overall corporate mission. Companies develop labels for their people-advocating strategies like "putting people first"[1] or "people before strategy."[2]

Putting people first is certainly a worthy goal. A company that focuses on the assets inherent in its human resources will foster an internal business environment that is attentive to the talent that lies within the organization and to ways in which this talent's full potential can be realized. However, organizations have finite resources and, as such, they must decide which people-oriented priorities are most important to them and how these priorities can be properly implemented. What are the key determinants of an organization's integral "people strategy?"

Some organizations may construct new compensation models, thereby placing great emphasis on rewarding excellent work performance through monetary incentives. Other organizations may

1

augment benefit packages. These strategies are important, but research has shown that extrinsic rewards often fail to motivate excellent job performance as effectively as the more intrinsic rewards of work.[3]

Management human relations: the most crucial "people strategy"

> ...the most crucial element of a corporate "people strategy" should be developing the human relations skills practiced by managers with their direct reports, in group and individual interactions.

Our experience is that when people feel good about the organization that employs them, when they feel excited about coming to work every day, their positive, inspired attitude typically is more attributable to the healthy, respectful relationships that exist between themselves and the individuals leading them, i.e., their managers. The same can be said in a "team-building" context; teams function well when a number of dynamics are in effect, but the most important of these involves the team leader's interpersonal behaviors. Indeed, *the most crucial element of a corporate "people strategy" should be developing the human relations skills practiced by managers with their direct reports, in group and individual interactions.* This principle of organizational management serves as the central theme behind our *SOLID people management* training model.

Theory X and Theory Y

Human relations practices have held a significant position of importance in organizational management theory for well over a half-century.

One of the most famous writings about management human relations during this time period came from Douglas McGregor, who coined the terms "*Theory X*" and "*Theory Y.*" These terms have become well-integrated into management nomenclature.

"The Human Side of Enterprise,"[4] in which McGregor's "*Theory X*" and "*Theory Y*" thesis appears, has resonated throughout the ranks of management for over forty years (it was published in 1960). It strikes a chord with managers because they relate to the distinction between leadership styles that McGregor proposes. The distinction continues to be relevant even now.

McGregor's seminal work has helped clarify a set of values that organizations hold about how they interact with their people. The general management human relations principles in *Theory X* and *Theory Y* may be widely known, but it is useful to learn what McGregor actually describes in his writings. He essentially elucidates a stark attitudinal difference in the way to approach leading others. *Theory X* assumes:

- The average human being has an inherent dislike of work.
- People avoid work when they can.
- Because of their dislike for work, most people must be controlled and threatened before they will work hard enough.
- The average human:
  o prefers to be directed;
  o dislikes responsibility;
  o is unambiguous; and
  o desires security above everything.[5]

In contrast to the *Theory X* approach to managing others, McGregor describes a more people-friendly and empowering approach to leading others that he labels *Theory Y. Theory Y* assumes:

- The expenditure of physical and mental effort in work is as natural as play or rest.
- Control and punishment are not the only ways to make people work. People will direct themselves if they are committed to the aims of the organization.
- If a job is satisfying, then the result will be commitment to the organization.
- The average person learns, under proper conditions, not only to accept but to seek responsibility.
- Imagination, creativity, and ingenuity can be used to solve work problems by a large number of employees.
- Under the conditions of modern industrial life, the intellectual potentialities of the average person are only partially utilized.[6]

Since *Theory X* and *Theory Y* present such polar opposites to attitudes about management, many leaders actually integrate components from each in the way they supervise people and departments. But the implication behind McGregor's management thesis remains highly relevant: people are assets that can be nurtured for the benefit of the organization.

Ron Willingham, author and Chairman of management consulting firm Integrity Systems, uses a term he calls "The People Principle" to describe how important human relations approaches are to organizational management.[7] Willingham's advocates that *"People are more important than processes."*[8] He bemoans the wasted resources spent in American industry on technology and organizational strategies that ignore tapping into human potential factors to improve productivity.

There is much of McGregor's *Theory Y* value set in Willingham's "People Principle." Willingham states his beliefs about managing people as follows:

> "All people have unlimited potential that has been largely unrecognized and untapped. When discovered and accessed, this potential can lead them to far greater levels of productivity than they ever imagined, causing them to feel better about themselves and enjoy life more."[9]

Managers that share these values can set up a truly ideal leadership scenario for an organization—*Theory Y* managers would be able to move forward with strategic initiatives in an ever-more competitive business environment, while empowered, dedicated and motivated employees make a significant contribution to existing operations.

The case for Theory Y in management science

Industrial psychologists have scientifically validated the hypothesis that effective managers have greater levels of psychological health. This makes the utmost sense. Most of us recognize that individuals who can form effective, role-congruent relationships with other people—at home, in the community and at work—are more successful in life, have greater ego strength and communicate more effectively than those who cannot form such relationships. Intuitively, it feels correct that managers with a knack for human relations tend to be individuals with higher levels of psychological health, and vice versa. In fact, this relationship has been tested in organizational research and found to be the case.

Dr. Abraham Maslow, a pioneer in the study of organizational behavior, the developer of the famous theory that describes the hierarchy of worker's needs in their jobs (*see Chapter 11 for a further description of this theory*) and, incidentally, a key contributor to McGregor's thinking as he developed his *Theory X* and *Theory Y* approaches to management, performed extensive research on the relationship between effective leadership and psychological health. In reviewing his and others' relevant research, Dr. Maslow finds that if a list of psychological health characteristics is made, each of these characteristics is predicted to be found in a greater degree in better managers than in poorer managers.[10]

Maslow goes on to note that if we look at the person who is best suited to be a leader—that is, the one who is best suited actually to solve the problem or to pursue a task successfully, the one who is most perceptive about the objective requirements of a situation, the person who tends to be psychologically healthier—that person is less likely to get "a kick out of" being able to order people around in a bossy manner. "Doing so just does not give them gratification," Maslow suggests.[11]

So Maslow is not only connecting psychological health to effective management in general, he is also addressing issues about the use of power and control over subordinates. The implications of these empirical findings are clear. Successful and more psychologically healthy managers are comfortable with interpersonal negotiation and mediation, teamwork, and staff empowerment. As importantly, it is evident in research studies that tyrannical, dictatorial and abusive managers not only are less effective, but they demonstrate individual psychological needs that run counter to organizational needs.

It is apparent, then, that psychologically healthier managers would tend to be *Theory* Y-type managers, since domination and control are less important to them than they are to *Theory* X-type managers. And if psychologically healthier managers are better managers, then people-oriented, *Theory* Y-type managers are better managers.

A clear connection is evident between the more successful and productive *Theory Y* management style and the six indispensable competencies we present in our *SOLID people management* model. *Theory Y*-type managers prioritize management human relations aptitudes because these skills help establish a respectful and empowering tone for the supervisory relationship. Throughout our *SOLID people management* model, there is evidence of an underlying *Theory Y* approach to establishing productive relationships, problem-solving and people development. This book can help managers who have led others using a more *Theory X*-type of style begin to transform their leadership approach toward *Theory Y*-type values. The information we present also can help managers with an affinity to *Theory Y*-type values build skills to make themselves more effective in this leadership style.

2

The Concept of <u>People</u> <u>Management</u> Skills

Consider the following:

- Soon after the tragedy of September 11, 2001, President Bush appointed Governor Tom Ridge to head up a new national homeland security department. Commenting on this appointment, former Philadelphia Mayor Ed Rendell said that the choice of Governor Ridge was excellent because of his inherent *"people management skills."*
- In reading management help wanted ads in newspapers or a recruitment postings over the Internet for leadership positions, many descriptions of the job requirements include something about the candidate needing to demonstrate *"leadership people skills."* These skills are rarely defined or listed in the ads or job postings; the assumption is that individuals understand what having "leadership people skills" means.

It seems that "people management" and "leadership people skills" (identical concepts) have found their way into our everyday business vernacular. But just what are these "people management" skills that apply specifically to effective leadership? What does this term really mean? It is easy to state in a job description that a manager needs these skills, but doing so begs the issue of just what specific behaviors the employer is seeking. Workplace human interactions, which we assume are at the heart of people management skills, are extremely complex. How possible is it to define these skills with any degree of specificity?

> The *SOLID People Management* model we describe in this book focuses on human relations skills that <u>*generate quantifiable value*</u> for the organization, because these skills are inherent to superior leadership. The value to the organization of effective management human relations skills lies not simply in the benefits of competent communication but in the broader reinforcement of a *Theory Y* management *style*.

When considering the <u>general use</u> of the term "people skills", what comes to mind? Perhaps being a "good listener" an "effective communicator" is what you considered most important. But in the context of organizational management, there is a need to be much clearer about these aptitudes so that they can be measured and evaluated. The *SOLID People Management* model we describe in this book focuses on human relations skills that <u>*generate quantifiable value*</u> for the organization, because these skills are inherent to superior leadership. The value to the organization of effective management human relations skill lies not simply in the benefits of competent communication but in the broader reinforcement of a *Theory Y* management style.

A case example illustrates how a limited set of "people skills" may not prepare a supervisor for management challenges:

Bob R. is a highly performing salesman with the XYZ Company. Bob has great interpersonal skills. Bob is "in his element" performing sales prospecting, making connections with customers and assessing their needs. For two years, Bob has been XYZ company's top salesman. Ever since joining the firm he has outperformed other sales staff. Bob is a driven, self-confident man. He reads people very well in a sales context, and he is a skilled "closer." His customers enjoy associating with Bob. Customers like Bob as a person and remain very loyal to him despite attempts by competitors to be lured into other business arrangements.

Bob's sales results are so impressive that the firm considers ways to reward his efforts. They designate him as a sales manager responsible for two other salespeople in his territory. He continues to service his own accounts while taking on this limited supervisory role. He spends very little time with the sales staff assigned to him, and continues to outperform all other sales staff.

When a Director of Sales position opens up, the company selects Bob for this management role, again to reward his sales performance. Bob is now in charge of 25 sales staff. He is encouraged to assign his accounts to a sales person under his supervision. His responsibilities include motivating these salespeople, supporting their sales efforts and thereby growing sales revenues.

Within a month of Bob's promotion to Director of Sales, several sales staff people approach the Company President threatening to quit. The problem is Bob and his leadership style. His subordinates report that he is overbearing and very difficult to interact with. He overreacts to simple problems and levels criticism in a hurtful manner. He threatens

> peoples' jobs and creates a climate of intimidation. He pro-
> vides little support and guidance. The only time the sales
> staff can bear to be with him is when he accompanies them
> on a sales call and he focuses his attention on the customer
> and the sales issues.
>
> The company President calls Bob in and gives him a sup-
> portive yet firm message: "You are valuable to this com-
> pany, but it may not be in a supervisory role. We need you
> to modify your management approach, otherwise changes
> will need to be made."

The Company put itself in the unenviable position of jeopardizing its
employment relationship with a person responsible for a considerable
amount of the Company's sales revenue. Bob's promotion to Director
of Sales assumed that sales-oriented people skills translated well into
sales management people skills. The fact is that once Bob assumed a
management role, he needed to employ a wider range and different
types of skills necessary to succeed in that role.

The people skills that made Bob a success as a salesman certainly have
some relevance to the types of skills he will need to succeed as a sales
manager. However, when one assumes a management role, not only do
a broader set of skills become relevant but the people skills that Bob
owns need to be applied to different types of challenges. As an example,
coaching others to communicate well with customers and solving subordinates' performance problems are different skills than communicating well or resolving problems with outside customers on one's own.

Can a healthier, more empowering *Theory Y*-type management style be
taught? Further, can "people skills" be developed in those who have
relied on analytical or more technical aptitudes to get ahead in an
organization? The answer to both questions, we believe, is a qualified

"Yes"—especially when the organization values these behaviors and reinforces them in their day-to-day management decision-making and manpower planning. Managers are more likely to see the importance of and make progress in their human relations competencies when the corporate message is, "Take care of your people, bring out the value in the human capital under your authority, and you will succeed in this organization."

People skills require emotional as well as mental dexterity, but they are introduced and practiced much as other occupational techniques are: by learning the fundamental techniques—like those we are about to describe to you—and by practicing them. Certainly, human relations aspects of one's supervisory role can be less natural and more challenging for some than others, and there is an "art" to exercising highly refined people skills, but the techniques we advocate in this book do build aptitudes that can make a significant and very positive impact in peoples' work and personal lives.

3

<u>Warning Signs</u> of People Management Problems

A variety of circumstances may draw attention to the need for organizations to address either their overall human relations practices or specific managers' problematic ways of interacting with those being supervised. The warning signs listed below should motivate organizations to remedy these situations. To not do so is to accept the prevalence of the many associated problems: wasted resources, manpower shortages, poor morale, divided team loyalties and more. Indeed, our model of essential management human relations practices is built on assessments and corrective planning performed after things have gone wrong—sometimes very wrong—within an organization. Like physicians whose experience observing advanced disease states leads them to conclusions about best practices for developing a healthy lifestyle, we base our approach to building *SOLID people management* competencies on years of observing costly outcomes when these skills are inadequate. We believe in the adage about the ounce of prevention being better than a pound of cure. Training and re-training are the keys to turning the following problematic situations around. These warning signs should be far less prevalent once managers incorporate the essential human relations practices we advocate in our *SOLID people management* training model.

- *Higher than average turnover:* As the saying goes, "People don't leave their jobs, they leave their managers." When inordinate amounts of turnover exist in an organization or in a particular group, it may be that leadership is alienating valuable staff members. The resulting frustration can compel these individuals to quit the organization. High turnover rates increase a business's manpower expenses, create the opportunity for lower or erratic team performance and add new burdens to what is often a fragile relationship between remaining employees and managers. An analysis of exit interview data relating to the departing employees' relationships with their supervisors can be useful in identifying problematic communication practices or specific development needs for managers experiencing the highest rates of turnover.

- *Difficulty filling open positions from within:* Staff turnover creates job openings that must be filled to keep operations running smoothly. Hiring from within the organization is often the organization's first and most cost-effective option. When a manager develops a reputation as someone who is difficult to work for or work with, these positions can be difficult to fill from within. This forces an organization to conduct an external search, which invariably is more expensive and time-consuming.

- *Level and types of disputes that Human Resources staff members are called upon to mediate:* When specific managers' human relations skills are deficient, decisions are often communicated poorly. Miscommunication can generate a sense of inequity or unfairness about these decisions, leading to disputes that tend to reach Human Resources Departments because they relate to the application of written company policies or procedures. Human Resources and other organizational resources are drawn into "putting out fires" caused less by the decisions made but more by their timing and the way they were communicated to affected parties. Time, resources and organizational energy are devoted to mediating disputes rather than formulating and implementing business plans. When such dispute arbitrations occur frequently within a certain department or group under a particular supervisor, a problem may be evident in that particular supervisor's relationship-building skills.

- *Employees file grievances or lawsuits against a manager and the company:* When disputes are not or can not be mediated at the Human Resources Department level, then employees may "push" their issues further through filing grievances (primarily in a union-organized environment) and/or lawsuits. Both of these more formal dispute resolution mechanisms put a considerable amount of strain on the organization's time and resources. Some grievances or lawsuits are filed more for annoyance value, and can be seen as part and parcel of employing people in a business. But frequent impasses in resolving workplace disputes between managers and subordinates can point to a need to address communication and conflict management skills among supervisory staff.

- *Performance reviews are challenged:* A performance review should be just that—a <u>review</u> of information a supervisor provides to a direct report on an ongoing basis about the direct report's performance. Yet the performance review process can become contentious when sub-standard human relations skills fuel disagreements and acrimony. As we will discuss in Chapter 10, there are ways to present "bad news" that promote moving forward on a positive note. When this skill is lacking, the human relations environment can be highly "touchy" and argument-laden.

- *Company policies and procedures are sidestepped because certain departments and/or their leaders are deemed "difficult to work with":* Like it or not, workflows within organizations often follow the path of least resistance. Certain managers or departments can develop a reputation for territoriality, for being "difficult to work with." For expedience sake, other parts of the organization may try to find ways to avoid encountering the interpersonal problems that they find inherent in working with particular managers or the departments they run. This sidestepping usually causes other operational problems, as established rules get broken or acceptable procedures overlooked. Conflicts develop that need to be mediated. The person responsible for the "logjam" or "bottleneck" is often someone whose "people skills" are problematic.

- *Schisms or cliques are evident within a department:* When "cliquish" groups develop within organizations, intradepartmental cooperation and teamwork can be compromised. A sense that particular leaders "play favorites" can lead to interpersonal conflicts within groups that adversely affect group performance.

The following are additional <u>direct signs</u> that an intervention is needed with specific managers about how they interact with people under their supervision:

- 360 degree multi-rater assessments (*defined further in Chapter 7*) demonstrate problems in human relations aspects of a particular manager's performance;
- Accusations of sexual or verbal harassment are made about a manager or managers;
- Incidents occur when a particular manager loses his or her "cool" to the extent that it affects team morale or causes "scenes" that make others uncomfortable;
- Unsettled interdepartmental disputes involving a particular manager paralyze operations;
- A particular manager has highly visible off-the-job personal problems, such as legal troubles like being arrested for DWI or for incidents of domestic violence.

Keeping tabs on these manifestations of deficiencies in management human relations can help organizations address problems at an earlier stage in order to proactively initiate corrective training plans. Across-the-board leadership training may be indicated when problems are more systemic in nature, while individualized coaching may be the most prudent intervention when most of the more serious problems appear to stem from a specific manager or group of managers. In either case, action needs to be taken to address troublesome warning signs of human relations-oriented management problems. Leadership development training and/or individualized coaching are certainly sound, prudent and cost-effective actions for organizations to take in addressing these problems.

Our *"SOLID People Management"* Pyramid: A Model of Organizational and Personal Human Relations Competencies

Introducing Our "*S.O.L.I.D.* Pyramid*" Model

How To Use the "*S.O.L.I.D.* Pyramid*" Model to Build People Management Competencies

* = $\underline{S}$kills for $\underline{O}$rganizational $\underline{L}$eadership and $\underline{I}$ndividual $\underline{D}$evelopment
(S.O.L.I.D. People Management)

4

Introducing Our *"S.O.L.I.D. Pyramid"* Model

Most often, client organizations retain our management human relations consulting services when the "red flags" delineated in the previous chapter are evident. Something is "wrong." Organizations want their management human relations problems fixed. Our model includes six practices—*practicing empathy, expanding self-awareness, following "Golden Rule" principles, maintaining proper boundaries/setting appropriate limits, criticizing artfully* and *flexing to accommodate different people styles*—that are the common, consistent focus of our management coaching efforts. Actually, these practices are much more than competencies that merely keep managers out of trouble—they blend together, forming an integrated set of skills for organizational leadership and individual development.

These six practices are by no means an all-inclusive list that compiles "everything a manager needs to know about relating better with the people they supervise and, insodoing, becoming a better person." Rather, they provide a framework—represented by a pyramid-shaped structure—by which individuals can focus their efforts to develop management human relations aptitudes. In our experience, improvement in these six people management competencies creates the opportunity to begin a process of fundamental and lasting positive change in managers' ability to lead people within any type of organizational setting.

Figure 1 on page 25 shows our model graphically. The model is represented by "building blocks" that form a <u>solid</u>, well-grounded pyramid. This representation visually reinforces the notion that while all the skills that we advocate are "essential," they can be arranged and prioritized in a sensible order.

The bottom layer of our management human relations skills pyramid forms the base of the model. These are the "foundation" competencies: *practicing empathy*, *expanding self-awareness* and *following "Golden Rule principles."* These are the blocking and tackling that football coaches emphasize, the grip a golf pro goes over in the first lesson, the breathing techniques advocated by yoga instructors. They are practices that are intrinsic to the way managers manifest human relations talents. They help managers develop into fundamentally better people.

In a middle layer, two specific supervisory people skills—*maintaining proper boundaries* and *criticizing artfully*—build upon the three core skills at the foundation and are applied to common management challenges. To be most useful, our model needs to be more than an exploration of widely admired, foundation-layer skills. We want to emphasize approaches to management human relations challenges that actually test one's empathy, emotional self-awareness and ability to apply golden Rule principles.

Why did we choose these two particular challenges to expand upon in our model? The fact is that in a significant percentage of the cases for which we have provided coaching services, two problems recur again and again:

1. Managers compromise their authority through bad judgments, inappropriate behavior or ineffective limit-setting with respect to their interpersonal relationships at work.
2. Managers alienate people through their frustrated reactions to subpar performance. Their criticism is intolerant and hurtful. They deliver bad news or critical opinions in a way that undermines rather than reinforces subordinates' morale and team spirit.

Since these problems are brought to our attention most frequently, they must: a) pose difficulties for individuals—or at least some of them—who are in positions of authority; and b) have widespread ramifications within the organization when these skills are lacking. In the spirit of developing a model with <u>relevance</u> to day-to-day management practice (*see Premise 3 in our Introduction*), we believe it is essential to describe these two competencies and ways to develop them.

At the top of the pyramid, we present a type of "capstone" aptitude that is presented less in the context of preventing common problems and more in the context of advanced skill development. It is a skill that allows you to optimize your relationships with all sorts of people. We refer to this practice as *flexing to different people styles*. This skill reinforces the value of being adaptable to the unique characteristics of other people. It takes advantage of managers' sincere interest in people, the product of which is an investment in finding ways to develop performance-enhancing rapport with those under the managers' supervision.

Our pyramid building-block image is purposeful and intrinsic to our teaching/coaching process. In a pyramid, the base is the broadest layer. It supports all the layers above it. Pyramids are rather simple structures, but highly <u>solid</u>. Sturdiness is an attractive feature to a business model, because it is important to build things that last and that one can add to with additional layers as needed.

Earlier in this Chapter, we mentioned that our model involves acquiring <u>s</u>kills for <u>o</u>rganizational <u>l</u>eadership and <u>i</u>ndividual <u>d</u>evelopment. When you put the acronym together, it spells *SOLID*—just the image we are conveying through our model's pyramid shape. *SOLID People Management* requires building a strong foundation, a base of personal traits that makes managers better people. These traits then reinforce refined judgment skills, diplomacy, perspective and control over detrimental impulsive behavior—so important to communicating effectively at work and, ultimately, to success in one's career. They also reinforce dynamic adaptability to an ever-changing, inherently diverse workforce.

FIGURE 1

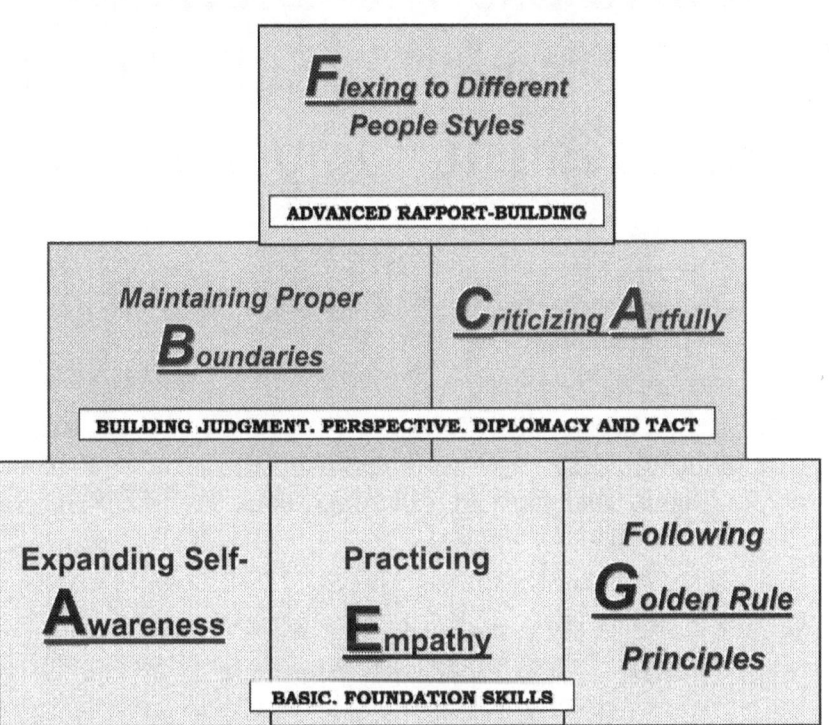

"SOLID* PYRAMID" MODEL OF PEOPLE MANAGEMENT COMPETENCIES

*F*lexing *to Different People Styles*

ADVANCED RAPPORT-BUILDING

Maintaining Proper **B**oundaries

Criticizing **A**rtfully

BUILDING JUDGMENT. PERSPECTIVE. DIPLOMACY AND TACT

Expanding Self-**A**wareness

Practicing **E**mpathy

Following **G**olden Rule *Principles*

BASIC. FOUNDATION SKILLS

* Skills for Organizational Leadership and Individual Development

5

How To Use The "*S.O.L.I.D. Pyramid*" Model To Build People Management Competencies

There are two primary ways to use this book to build *SOLID people management* competencies:

1. *The self-help approach:* The six practices we espouse *are purposefully framed as action-oriented improvement goals*, rather than simply readings on management skill topics. Thus, a self-help approach can be undertaken by following specific behavioral recommendations. The "Coaching Yourself in *SOLID* People Management Competencies" section of this book encourages you to log your responses to specific, numbered questions we pose. Keeping this log helps you document your ideas and insights from practicing the model's six essential management human relations practices. The log can serve as a point of reference for future evaluations of your progress in attaining our model's essential management human relations competencies.

   To conduct such a self-help plan, you may also wish to do the following:

a) Select the human relations practice(s) that require(s) the most attention from you, based on feedback you have received or personal skill inventorying you have undertaken, for more extensive developmental work.

b) After re-reading our chapter on the skill you wish to develop, research more about what the experts say about the skill from the original source material we cite in the References for each Chapter. The material we have chosen is highly practical and readable. We shied away from more academic material that can be difficult to read through quickly. Authors of these source materials intended their information to be absorbed by professional managers. We believe we have selected a group of management skill-building materials that serve as a very useful complement to understanding and implementing our management development model.

c) We have developed a means for you to have a 360 multi-rater assessment (*see Chapter 7 for an explanation of this tool*) performed through an Internet website. For a modest fee, you can have an assessment conducted just like those we do for our corporate clients. After the assessment is complete, a comprehensive report of findings is developed for you to keep. Instructions on how to perform your own multi-rater feedback profile are included in Appendix B.

Again, if you choose to move forward with this option, you will need to be prepared to ask others to rate you on your leadership human relations skills. Start considering which peers, supervisors and subordinates you might want to engage in the process of providing you with feedback.

2. *The professional coaching approach*: The book can also be used in conjunction with an individualized management coaching process.

Hire a coach and work with him or her as you make your way through the content and exercises we present.

Appendix A provides an overview of management coaching and the respective responsibilities of the management coach and the client manager who take part in this training process. It will help you better understand this training method and preparing you for what to expect when you hire a coach.

Coaches use different techniques and approaches, and they have different priorities and fundamental experience. For this purpose—developing your management people skills—you will want to select a coach that agrees with our *SOLID People Management* model and is comfortable with the exercises in the next section. You probably do not want to hire a coach whose main focus is on things like making life choices, finding happiness, etc. For present purposes, the best choice is someone who works with managers on their leadership problems or challenges. If you have any difficulties locating a coach, feel free to contact us (*see Foreword for our contact information*).

Prepare to make positive changes: the next step is yours

A manager with an openness and interest in skill development in the human relations area will have much to absorb. Practicing new skills invariably involves recognizing the difficulty of breaking old habits or patterns of behavior that have proven to be self-defeating. But with the reinforcement of the *SOLID People Management* techniques outlined in this book and, if you so choose, with the support of a professional management coach, real positive change will occur.

The Six Essential "S.O.L.I.D." People Management Practices

Practicing Empathy

Expanding Self-Awareness

Following "Golden Rule" Principles

Maintaining Proper Boundaries/
Setting Appropriate Limits

Criticizing Artfully

Flexing to Different People Styles

6

Practicing Empathy

"Do your listening skills, life experiences and intuitions about human nature come together and help you read people? Could any skill be more valuable in the workplace?"
From Tip #17, "Practice Empathy,"
in "20 Communication Tips @ Work" by Dr. Eric Maisel[1]

Introduction to Practicing Empathy

The most central and foundation-supporting "building block" within our pyramid-shaped *SOLID People Management* model is *practicing empathy*. Most experts in leadership development note in very specific terms that empathy is a crucial component of effective management. Empathy is seen as a critical communication <u>skill</u> that becomes engrained in a people-oriented management <u>style</u>. The more adept you become at communicating empathetically, at sensing what others are thinking and feeling, the better equipped you will become at knowing what messages to send and how to frame them.[2]

In this chapter, we provide some guidelines for practicing empathy in an organizational management context.

Defining empathy, and its applicability to managing others at work

The term empathy derives from the Greek word **"empatheia"** or feeling into; the ability to perceive the subjective experience of another person. For our purposes, empathy is defined simply as:

> **"The capacity to _understand_ and _respond effectively_ to the _unique experience of another_."**

Certainly managers are required to "_understand_" a number of things about the people who work for them. They need to understand, for example, their direct reports' skill levels and competencies, their training needs, etc.

"_Responding effectively_" to situations that present themselves at work is also an essential component of managing others. Judgment about which response to employ in different situations is a crucial part of managing people.

The skill of empathy adds another dimension to the ability to simply understand and respond to people and work circumstances. Empathy focuses on communicating with others in a way that makes them feel uniquely understood. It involves an ability to assess what is going on within people they supervise—the "_unique circumstances_" of these people"—and to do so in a way that the employee feels affirmed, validated and appreciated. Empathy is an essential component of "reading" people and expressing an interest in what they are experiencing. Exercising empathy at work is a recognition that listening to and caring for people matters in the performance of the organizational mission.

The difference between "sympathy" and "empathy"

It is important to have an appreciation for how the terms "sympathy" and "empathy" relate to each other. The distinction between these two seemingly analogous terms lies in the difference between "feeling for" someone (sympathy) versus "feeling with" someone (empathy). The sympathetic response feels for someone out of an orientation to one's own experience. The empathic response feels with the person, with an orientation to the other person's unique circumstances. Sympathy is a form of agreement, rather than an exploration of feeling—it is emotionally distant. Empathy, on the other hand, is emotionally connecting. Empathic listeners feel others' pain, their joy, grief and frustration. Sympathy leaves the person feeling supported but not uniquely understood.

Consider your own experiences receiving an empathic response

To understand what empathy is and its importance to human relationships of all kinds, consider an interaction or series of interactions with another person when you felt:

o   Your words had been listened to and truly understood.
o   Engaged rather than simply heard in a conversation.
o   Pleased that the interaction took place because of it created a feeling of connection to the other person.
o   A wish to have additional opportunities for an interaction with this person.

The interaction you chose may have been part of a loving relationship or friendship. Obviously, empathy is a key component of intimacy with others, because of empathy's power in connecting people to one another.

The interaction you chose may also have been a professional one. Teachers, academic supervisors, mentors, clergy or caregivers are common examples of the types of individuals who can model empathy in professional relationships. Either way—whether you chose a personal or professional relationship as an example of empathic communication—it is important that you have experienced empathy in action.

When these empathic experiences occur frequently in one's life, one has a model or several models to use as a frame of reference in developing one's own natural empathic abilities. For those with a paucity of past empathic experiences in their private and/or work lives, developing empathy skills can be a real challenge. It is—as this Chapter's title implies—a skill that needs to be *practiced*, again and again, in human relationships both at home and at work. It is certainly easier to emulate the skill when you have good models of empathy in your life.

At work, we encourage you to make an effort to observe peers that you sense have a natural ability to connect on a feeling level with their subordinates, and who are more effective in their management role as a result. Make note of their techniques. Compare the techniques you see them use with those we share in the remainder of this Chapter.

Guidelines for practicing empathy

There are two interrelated areas of empathy skill development.

1. Empathic listening
2. Expressing empathy

The latter requires the former. A manager needs to understand the value of hearing what others say, and of doing so with involvement and feeling. The manager then can focus on how to express empathy back to others in verbal interaction more naturally and helpfully.

Empathic listening

"To 'listen' another's soul into life, into a condition of disclosure and discovery, may be the greatest service that any human being ever performs for another."[3] *Douglas Steere*	"Empathic listening gets inside another person's frame of reference. You look out through it, you see the world the way they see the world, you understand their paradigm, you understand how they feel."[4] *Steven Covey*

For managers, listening with empathy requires giving up a self-centered view of work and of one's status in an organization. Giving up a self-centered orientation allows a manager to participate fully in the other person's experience. The art of listening requires discipline and energy, directed externally rather than internally. Managers need to evaluate how much time they spend talking (often behavior that is self-oriented) and how much time they spend listening (most often behavior that is externally-oriented).

Now, let's review some key points about empathic listening:

Empathic listeners do **not**:

• Spend most of the time rehearsing what they intend to say once it is their turn to talk during the process of hearing other people speak.
• Tend to rush in and fix things with their good advice.

- Pick up certain phrases or pieces of the statements from others and ignore the rest.
- Make up their minds before they hear the entire scope of the other person's words.
- Connect everything another person says to their own experiences, not honoring the uniqueness of the other person's thoughts or feelings.

---

6 ways to build fundamental listening skills

1. **Eliminate distractions:** put phone on voice mail, close the door to the office, put away things you are working on.
2. **Be comfortable with silence:** allowing silent interludes between expressions of issues, facts or feelings conveys patience, understanding and a willingness to let a story unfold.
3. **Maintain good eye contact:** this helps demonstrate an interest and connectedness to the speaker.
4. **Clear your mind and focus on hearing what the speaker is saying:** Other work issues need to be set aside during the discussion, to allow the manager to listen effectively.
5. **Avoid snap judgments:** Engrained judgmental attitudes can thwart an effort to gain an understanding of another's unique circumstances.
6. **If you keep notes, write down only key points:** Maintain optimum eye contact. Excessive writing interferes with the ability to listen to everything that is being said, and it can be a way of maintaining an emotional distance that impedes empathic listening.

Empathic listeners <u>do</u>:
- Make a conscious effort to respond to what is left unspoken.
- Set aside their biases and prejudices.
- Connect with another person's emotions without getting too carried away with them.

o Give people a chance to explain themselves fully.
o Focus and concentrate on the conversation without distraction.

In essence, you need to prepare yourself to listen more empathetically:

> "If you can let down your defenses, quiet the chatter in your mind, and turn all your attention to the person opposite you, you will suddenly know what her words and actions mean."[5]

As its definition conveys, empathy stems from feeling with the other person. Empathic listening emphasizes an interest in fully understanding the other person's feelings and viewpoints. In his classic book *On Becoming a Person*[6], psychologist Carl Rogers provides an exercise in empathic listening during a conflict:

> "The next time you get in an argument…just stop the discussion for a moment and for an experiment, institute this rule. 'Each person can speak up for himself only *after* he has first restated the ideas and feelings of the previous speaker accurately, and to that speaker's satisfaction.' You see what this would mean. It would simply mean that before presenting your own point of view, it would be necessary for you to really achieve the other speaker's frame of reference—to understand his thoughts and feelings so well that you can summarize them for him. Sounds simple, doesn't it? But if you try it you will discover it is one of the most difficult things you have ever tried to do. However, once you have been able to see the other's point of view, your own comments will have to be drastically revised. You will find the emotion going out of the discussion, the differences being

reduced, and those differences which remain being of a rational and understandable sort."

In a similar vein, Dr. Steven Covey devotes an entire section of his highly popular book "The 7 Habits of Highly Effective People"[7] to principles of empathic communication. He re-states Dr. Rogers' message this way:

"Seek first to understand, then to be understood."

This, Dr. Covey insists, is the key to effective interpersonal communication and conflict mediation.

"When you listen with empathy to another person, you give that person psychological air. And after that vital need is met, you can then focus on influencing and problem solving."[8]

If one practices communicating at work in a way that *seeks first to understand then to be understood,* more empathic interactions are bound to take place. The obstacles to developing this "people skill" stem mostly from a reluctance within the manager to re-orient his or her communication style away from a focus on one's own priorities and interests. To understand someone else's unique circumstances, one must be "other-oriented." Practicing empathy involves getting beyond self-interest and exercising an interest in other people and what is going on with them. Once this "other-oriented" manner of interacting with people begins to take hold, the manager is preparing him or herself to begin to express empathy verbally through words, inquiries and a concern for the feelings of those with whom he or she interacts.

Expressing empathy

Let's review how empathy is expressed to another person. Empathic listening certainly begins the process of expressing empathy to the other person. Empathy is expressed during listening when the other person feels heard. However, listening alone does not create an empathic interaction. One must respond to the other person to express empathy, to make him or her feel uniquely understood. Here are some suggestions listed by Dr. Arthur P. Ciaramicoli and Kathrine Ketcham, co-authors of the book "The Power of Empathy."[9]

- ♦ Ask open-ended questions
- ♦ Slow down
- ♦ Pay attention to your body
- ♦ Learn from the past
- ♦ Let the story unfold
- ♦ Set limits

Ask open-ended questions:

Asking effective questions helps managers perform their supervisory responsibilities. Almost by definition, empathic questions need to be open-ended. A "yes" or "no" answer simply does not allow for enough information to be shared that will facilitate a deeper, more empathic response.

> *Hint!* Build in openings like "Tell me more about" and "Explain to me" at the beginning of your inquiries at work. These openings set a tone of shared interest and empathy to work discussions. It actually changes the discussion into a "Statement and Answer" format rather than a "Question and Answer" give-and-take. The "Statement and Answer" format can be considerably less threatening to the person with whom you are talking, and it facilitates more non-defensive responses.

Slow down:

Expressing empathy takes time. The workplace can't always accommodate this need to slow down. The demands on one's time at work can be overwhelming. A manager often operates in a hectic matrix of cross-functional communication and shared responsibilities. Some interactions between managers and their direct reports need to be brief, concise and time-limited. However, just as managers should not rush into important decisions that require substantial information, managers also have to be sensitive to the need to create opportunities for interactions with others that can proceed at their own pace. Unrealistic time restrictions can subvert an exchange when one wants to express empathy. Clearly, when a person is sending strong signals to a manager of their frustration, anxiety or anger, the interaction that takes place to resolve problems cannot be rushed.

> *Hint!* It is not always the manager's busy schedule that forces a need to "slow down" and to create the kind of substantive, uninterrupted exchange that allows one to exercise empathy. At times, it is the manager's direct report that needs to be told "Slow down." Some more difficult employees may thrive on a stressful, chaotic environment with unreasonable time demands, because it is a work culture that fosters disagreements and resentments. A manager may need to "pull the plug" on the charged-up, hectic work environment from time to time, and insist on a slower paced discussion that allows the manager to understand and respond empathically to the work dilemmas at hand.

Pay attention to your body:

The body is an excellent barometer of one's feeling state. When practicing empathy, "step back" mentally from time to time and consider your own body's messages. Are you tense (tight muscles, stiff)? Agitated (excited, racing pulse, flushed)? Bored or increasingly distant (not concentrating, sleepy, yawning, eyes wandering)? The body can provide you with signals that allow you to re-focus or acknowledge an affective reaction to the content of the discussion. When appropriate, note your body signals to the other person. Sharing one's physical response to what is occurring can facilitate the inclusion of emotional components into the discussion's content. This can lead to greater human connectedness and improved mutual understanding.

Learn from the past:

We all bring our own experiences to interpersonal interactions. We are all observers of human behavior in many ways. Some of these experiences and observations can help us understand what another person is telling us, and what may have been left unsaid. The power of empathy can be especially strong when we base an empathic response on previous experience—especially a response that makes note of what has been left unsaid—and it "hits the mark" in the person with whom we are communicating.

Let the story unfold:

As we slow down and avoid snap judgments, we create an environment that lets the other person's story unfold. The empathic communicator asks him/herself, "Have I heard this person's full 'story'? Do I understand?" This is a skill that takes much practice. Indeed, it is an art to determine that a story that one is listening to is not full or complete, and to have the patience to allow it to unfold. Many of us have an urge or compulsion to move forward with solutions before all the story is told.

Set limits:

Setting limits sounds like good, general advice for managers, but what has it got to do with empathic communication? The answer involves using empathy to help the other person focus on what it is that needs to be understood. When someone's thoughts seem disconnected or "scattered," the empathic communicator will need to confront this artfully, and move the person back to the true "unique circumstances" that seek empathic understanding and responsiveness. Empathy is strongest when the other party acknowledges that the listener will not be easily swayed or will not follow distracting ideas or behaviors.

Developmental stages in expressing empathy

Empathic listeners understand that one gains greater aptitude in "being empathic" as one moves through four common developmental stages in expressing empathy to other people.[10] These stages involve techniques that are widely used by caregivers and others with professional responsibilities requiring advanced empathic communication skills. Indeed, these techniques become second nature to these individuals in performing their duties. Managers would be well served by incorporating these techniques into their workplace interactions as well.

The first way to express that you are listening closely and wish to understand the other person is to *mimic content*. This means that you "ape" or copy the other person's words or last few words verbatim.

> <u>Example:</u>
> **Employee:** "The project deadline is only about a week away."
> **Manager practicing empathy may nod and say:** "Right. The deadline is only about a week away." (Follow this with silence but active eye contact and continued engagement in the conversation.)
> **Employee:** "I don't know if we have the manpower to accomplish this project on time."
> **Manager practicing empathy:** "So, you don't think we have the manpower to get this project done on time."

This technique is simple to use. It is a rudimentary method of making the person feel heard, understood and responded to. Despite the simplistic nature of the technique, mimicking content can be useful—especially at an early stage in the conversation. As you are letting the story unfold, mimicking content and then remaining silent can give the other person the "psychological air" that Dr. Covey wrote about, and facilitate more useful sharing of problems and issues.

Let's move on to the second stage of empathic communication. It is a technique that entails *rephrasing the content*. Let's practice this on the same exchange as above.

> Employee: "The project deadline is only about a week away."
>
> Manager practicing empathy: "Yes, the deadline is really coming up quickly."
>
> Employee: "I just don't know if we have the manpower to accomplish this project on time."
>
> Manager practicing empathy: "So your sense is that we are a bit undermanned on this project, especially with the deadline only a week away."

Rephrasing the content is more responsive than pure mimicry, because it conveys more thoughtfulness in the response. This technique can make the listener appear more engaged, and willing to take in and synthesize the content of the discussion with attention to what has been said.

The third developmental stage of empathic communication is to *reflect the feeling*. By adding an attentiveness to their staff's feeling state, the manager moves closer to "feeling with" them, i.e., being empathic. Now the exchange might go like this:

> Employee: "The project deadline is only about a week away."
>
> Manager practicing empathy: "Sounds like you are very anxious about meeting this deadline."
>
> Employee: "I just don't know if we have the manpower to accomplish this project on time."
>
> Manager practicing empathy: "I'm hearing a lot of frustration that you don't have enough resources to work with to get this project done correctly. Tell me more about what's frustrating you."

Finally, the fourth stage of empathic communication combines the second and third stage—*rephrase the content and reflect the feeling*. This advanced skill uses active listening to hear the words and sense the feelings that are behind the words. Consider the greater opportunity for the employee feeling uniquely understood from the following exchange:

> **Employee:** "The project deadline is only about a week away."
>
> **Manager practicing empathy:** "We are getting closer to having to finish up this project, and you sound anxious about it."
>
> **Employee:** "I just don't know if we have the manpower to accomplish this project on time."
>
> **Manager practicing empathy:** "So it's your sense we are undermanned if we want to get this project done on time. That must be pretty frustrating for you. Tell me more about what is most frustrating to you."

Clearly, the ability to rephrase content <u>and</u> reflect feelings creates strong opportunities for empathic communication. The employee is likely to feel uniquely understood and responded to. The way is now paved for more open and mutual discussion about the reality of the employee's impressions and development of possible solutions.

Other management experts describe the importance of empathy within the process of conflict resolution. Empathy helps identify the "common ground" between two people, especially when this common ground involves feelings that have generated the dispute. Empathy is almost impossible to convey when the other person feels separated emotionally from you because of perceived differences. Conveying the sense that your respective experience and "take" on the problem at hand is quite similar can build bridges between people. When two people in a dispute find common ground, there is likely to be more emotional interest in finding a solution, rather than maintaining a posture of defiance.

Finding common ground is a technique that looks for points or issues where your respective experiences can be *blended*. **Blending** is another way of describing the essential skill involved in the "*rephrasing the content and reflecting the feeling*" recommendation described above. You are making an effort to connect what you are hearing and what you are feeling with what the other person is saying and appears to be feeling. Therapists and other caregivers often begin their empathic communications with the words, "It sounds like…" or "I'm hearing you say that…" These communication bridges are highly non-judgmental, they convey that you are listening closely and "feel with" the person. They reinforce behaviorally the guideline that empathic individuals, "Seek first to understand then to be understood."

How do managers express empathy in their leadership role? The examples of "practicing empathy" in a management role are virtually limitless. Certainly they do so when they lead individual and group meetings and seek input from others. They do so during periods of change. They do so in performance reviews, or when they are considering special requests. Empathy is crucial for resolving conflicts. It is a skill one uses day in and day out, at work and at home. It is a skill that becomes a style, a caring style used by those who manage others—and manage their own lives—with heart.

7

Expanding Self-Awareness

> *"Exceptional leaders look within first to enrich, enlighten and expand themselves...They use self-awareness to control themselves and ultimately have greater influence upon others."*

From "The 108 Skills of Natural Born Leaders" by Warren Blank[1]

Introduction

In the previous chapter, we explain how *practicing empathy* requires managers to be "other-oriented." However, one of the paradoxes of effective leadership is that in order to be "other-oriented," managers first must be comfortable with their own "inner life." Empathic leadership actually is rooted in self-assessment and self-awareness. An ability to understand and respond to the unique circumstances of another person (our definition of empathy) derives from a willingness to understand and respond to one's own needs, motivations, personality, strengths, weaknesses, ambitions and goals.

Self-awareness represents a subtle but very fundamental trait shared by effective leaders. Superior managers can spend as much time leading themselves as they do leading others. They know how important it is to investigate how one's inner self operates.

When managers exhibit a healthy inner curiosity—asking themselves "What makes me tick?"—it becomes very natural for them to extend this inquisitiveness to a genuine interest in others. Former United Nations Secretary General Dag Hammarskjold, who expertly mediated many international conflicts during the most tense periods of the Cold War era, summed up this issue very well when he said, "The more faithfully you listen to the voice within you, the better you will hear what is sounding outside."[2] In other words, self-awareness facilitates a better understanding of your environment and the people around you. The connection from self-awareness to highly refined, empathic people skills is logical and straightforward.

It is important for managers to appreciate the value not only of <u>having</u> self-awareness, but also of <u>expanding it over time</u>. Continuous self-discovery requires initiative, a willingness to dedicate time specifically to this purpose and an openness to self-improvement.

The process of expanding awareness is similar to following a regimen of physical and mental exercise. It prepares you for the challenges and exertions ahead. In the workplace context, self-awareness sharpens your instincts and helps fortify your overall business intuition. It provides a base from which effective day-to-day decisions are made and difficult problems are resolved.

The purpose of this chapter is to explain the relationship between expanding self-awareness and managing people well. We then go on to suggest ways in which you can optimize your self-awareness and integrate this activity into your management practice.

Bennis' Leadership Self-Awareness Formula

Dr. Warren Bennis, the eminent industrial psychologist, management theorist and leadership guru, framed a very sensible and intuitive connection between leaders' self-awareness and an aptitude for effective human interactions. The connection is presented as a tautological formula, describing a string of inter-related leadership traits that emanate from self-awareness.

"Self-awareness = Self-knowledge = Self-possession = Self-control = Self-expression"[3]

The Bennis formula begins with a connection between a leader's *self-awareness* and the result of self-awareness efforts, i.e., *self-knowledge*. This in turn breeds *self-possession*, a term that is synonymous with self-confidence, and then *self-control*.

Self-control is a personal attribute with a myriad of implications for effective management of people. Individuals with this competence:

o   Manage their impulsive feelings and distressing emotions well;
o   Stay composed, positive, and unflappable even in trying moments; and
o   Think clearly and stay focused under pressure.[4]

The value of managerial self-control manifests itself in the workplace in a virtually endless amount of ways. Certainly, this trait contributes to effective conflict management. Unproductive distractions are avoided. Work schedules are maintained. Planning is appreciated. Impulsiveness is checked.

These examples of self-control build the character of the individual manager and the level of trust within work groups. Indeed, people tend to admire managers who are able to stay composed and who operate well under pressure.

Thus, a connection that originates in self-awareness weaves its way into the ability of leaders to maintain their emotions on a stable, "even keel" despite stressful work circumstances. Bennis then completes the formula, positing that these inter-related traits culminate in competent *self-expression*. The full range of Bennis' formula is realized: self-awareness begets interactive management skills. Expertise in expressing oneself helps managers interact adroitly with the people around them. This skill prepares managers for the many human relations challenges they encounter in their position of leadership.

Emotional self-awareness

Dr. Daniel Goleman writes in his book "Working with Emotional Intelligence" that "self-awareness is the vital foundation skill for three emotional competencies: emotional awareness, accurate self-assessment and self confidence."[5] So, like Bennis, Goleman clarifies a connection between self-awareness, self-assessment (self-knowledge) and self-worth.

Goleman frames this connection from a negative perspective when he observes that "…a lack of self-awareness is an obstacle to realistic self-confidence…Self-confidence must be aligned with reality, and reality is a function of accurately perceiving one's skills and abilities."[6]

Goleman's perspective on management development emphasizes the value of emotional self-awareness. Attaining self-awareness requires attentiveness to one's moods and emotions. Emotional self-awareness helps us understand our inner life. It is a personal competency that translates directly into vital leadership qualities. According to Goleman, emotionally self-aware individuals:

o Know which emotions they are feeling and why;
o Realize the links between their feelings and what they think, do and say;

o   Recognize how their feelings affect their performance; and

o   Have a guiding awareness of their values and goals.[7]

Individuals with these attributes are in a position to perform an accurate self-assessment, which, Goleman believes, should include a "candid sense of our personal strengths and limits, a clear vision of where we need to improve, and the ability to learn from experience."[8]

People with a strong sense of self-worth, Goleman adds, are able to:

o   Present themselves with self-assurance; they have "presence;"

o   Voice views that are unpopular and go on out on a limb for that they believe is right;

o   Be decisive; they are capable of making sound decisions despite uncertainties and pressures.[9]

Managers with these traits are well on their way, in Goleman's view, to leading from the heart, to practicing empathy. So once again the connection is clarified between inner exploration—self-awareness and self assessment—and self confidence which paves the way for the kind of empathic interpersonal behavior that serves as the core feature of superior management human relations skills.

Accurate Self-Assessment

Part of a leader's efforts to develop self-awareness involves conducting an accurate self-assessment of his or her professional strengths and relative weaknesses. Such a self-assessment allows managers to target ways in which they can build upon what they do best and improve what they do less well.

We have already described the complementary nature of inner knowledge and of being able to understand and respond to the needs of others. Another aspect of self-awareness is that an interest in finding out what is "inside" is more often and more effectively gained through external interactions with others. It is common for others to see a characteristic or trait in a person that this person does not perceive on his or her own. Interactions between two people that include personal feedback of some sort is likely to uncover "blind spots," or aspects of one's behavior that others observe but about which the individual has little if any awareness. Usually, blind spots involve areas where personal improvement is warranted.

Uncovering blind spots

Some blind spots can be highly engrained. Our subconscious minds are prone to defense mechanisms like denial, or a tendency to avoid seeing things as they are. For some managers, these tendencies are highly maladaptive and can lead to considerable dysfunction in the groups they lead. These managers need concerted intervention from the outside to break through the defenses that the managers have established. This can be a fairly long and difficult process.

For other managers with an interest in expanding self-awareness, blind spots are simply part of "being human." Denial is not as evident as a simple lack of knowledge about how one's behavior impacts others. Managers who make a healthy effort to flesh out their blind spots are exhibiting an openness to others' impressions about aspects of their behavior.

Here's an example of a blind spot that involved a manager who is more open to uncovering blind spots and thereby improving his leadership effectiveness:

Case Example: The manager who changed his brand of humor

A finance manager at a hospital tries to use humor to create greater spirit amongst the team he leads. His objective is to create better interpersonal connections with his subordinates and with the clinical department heads he works with in committees. But his attempts at humor rarely create the laughter he anticipates. He wonders why, and seeks feedback from a peer. The peer points out that the humor he uses has a sarcastic edge to it, and some subordinates find his comedic style demeaning and condescending. Armed with this feedback, he eliminates these attempts at humor with his team. Instead, to lighten the mood at the start of a meeting he leads, he occasionally distributes a cartoon or comic from a magazine or newspaper that avoids sarcastic humor and is not likely to be offensive to anyone. He double checks the cartoon with the peer who gave him the feedback, prior to distributing it, to make sure that the comic or cartoon will be appropriate.

The result: in meetings where he distributes a cartoon, people laugh, smile and are more engaged as the meeting begins. Seeing this, he develops a file of funny comic strips and cartoons that he uses as it fits the agenda. People begin to look forward to his attempt at humor and admire his creativity.

The point of this case example is not that a blind spot existed in the hospital finance manager, or that this blind spot caused him problems in relations with other people. The point is that he sought out feedback to help him understand something about himself. Further, when he used feedback to try another behavior, he received positive reinforcement. People laughed *with him*, engaged by the pieces he distributed.

He was able to establish the kind of relaxed, team-building tone for staff meetings that he was looking to create. As a result, the meetings became more interactive and productive.

His interest in self-understanding, spurred by an intuition that told him people were not responding to him the way he expected, was rewarded with useful feedback and the reinforcement of new and clearly more successful behavior.

Seeking feedback is a constant quest

The hospital finance manager in our Case Example uses feedback to his advantage. He is a model for how being open to learn what others perceive about us can be very beneficial. He also models putting this feedback into action, by trying new behaviors in order to change negative perceptions that interfere with his professional practice.

Management consultant and author Warren Blank, in his book that outlines "The 108 Skills of Natural Born Leaders,"[10] makes several helpful suggestions to those who wish to engage in a continuous, daily effort to expand self-awareness. Blank encourages leaders to:

o *Hunt for feedback every day.*
o *Ask people above, below, across, and outside your organization for input on how you are doing.*
o *Seek feedback to confirm you are on the right track.*
o *Ask for reinforcement to clarify points for improvement.*
o *Take the pain that sometimes accompanies getting corrective feedback to help secure your power to grow.*
o *Commit to unadulterated excellence no matter how arduous the task. Get feedback on how well you measure up to that standard.*
o *Seek feedback that opens up the "blind spots" about your behavior.*

- o Seek feedback that indicates whether you should keep doing more of what you are doing.
- o Ask for "feed forward" information as well, to determine what you need to do differently in the future.
- o Always get specifics; ask for examples to understand the particular behavior that caused someone to assess your performance in a certain way.
- o Inquire about what others perceive as effective and ineffective actions.
- o Ask those providing feedback to show or tell you what could have been done differently.[11]

Consider the source

Even when the feedback you seek is more informal in nature and sought within one's daily routines, it is more productive and efficient if you do so in a planned, strategic way. We recommend that you consider the source of the feedback, and perform a degree of "screening" about what you hear.

All feedback is valid, and it is important to keep the feedback process as constructive as possible. Managers should always refrain from engaging in arguments about feedback they receive. But it is naïve to think that feedback is not influenced at all by others' personal agendas, unique perspectives on life, or their understanding (or lack thereof) about organizational dynamics, business imperatives and strategic decision-making in a competitive marketplace.

The ability to accept and weed through feedback becomes part of the "self-possession" that was in the middle of Bennis' formula. A cycle will develop in the midst of this feedback-seeking behavior, in which seasoned judgment, burgeoning self-confidence and a growing intuition about what feedback has merit all tie in to one another.

Here are a couple of suggestions for implementing a strategy that empowers your informal search for routine feedback at work and minimizes the chances that you will ignore useful feedback (thereby reinforcing detrimental blind spots):

- *Pre-select whose feedback would be most useful to solicit.* The individuals you select should have attributes that add value to their feedback, such as:
  - o **having a great deal of experience in an area in which you are requesting feedback,** since this experience adds credibility to the feedback;
  - o **a willingness to give honest, even critical feedback** if necessary, without fear of reprisal or concern that the feedback will somehow injure the relationship between the two of you;
  - o **someone you trust.** This implies that their feedback is not tainted by personal agendas. Instead, you count on their integrity in providing the feedback, and know that it is provided with your best interests—and the company's best interests—in mind.
- *Adjust the setting to the type of feedback you are soliciting.* By this, we mean that more personal feedback should be solicited in private, 1:1 interactions. Alternatively, there may be opportunities to solicit group input in the context of a team-building process. Such two-way communication is crucial for empowering teams and for improving the quality of the team's work.

More structured self-awareness tools

While informal feedback-seeking behavior is a way to continuously expand self-awareness, there are more formal ways for individuals or organizations to structure the feedback process. We will discuss three common and highly effective structured processes by which managers can expand their self-awareness:

1. 1:1 management coaching
2. 360° feedback appraisals
3. Psychological testing

We encourage not only that these tools be used, but that they be mixed and matched as situations dictate to achieve maximum effect. The mixing and matching of these methods facilitates a more comprehensive and tailored development process, which takes into account the level of self-awareness that exists and the severity of a manager's defensiveness and feedback-avoiding tendencies.

1:1 Management Coaching

A 1:1 management coach can be very helpful for leaders at any stage in their efforts to expand self-awareness. Management coaching can be particularly indicated in instances when managers are "well-defended," i.e., they have pervasive blind spots and are prone to avoid feedback. This leadership development tool is more individualized, interactive and dynamic. It provides intensive, personalized support and guidance through the feedback-receiving process. Feedback occurs in the form of structured 1:1 interactions with an experienced coach or mentor, that may include performing assessment interviews, holding goal-setting discussions, role-playing, working through ways to handle difficult situations and analyzing results of new behaviors. It is also a process for reviewing or evaluating feedback that managers have solicited themselves. The 1:1 management coaching process facilitates introspective analyses about factors important to growing managers' self-awareness, *particularly emotional self-awareness*. Coaches are trained to help managers understand their emotional lives, their "triggers" and other aspects of how their feelings influence behavior.

Management coaching is a popular option for organizations because:

o It is a less threatening and more supportive form of performance feedback. Most of us have been "coached" in some way—when we took part in athletics, perhaps in giving oral presentations, in maintaining fitness, etc. The term "coach" implies a resource that helps individuals or teams meet their full potential. This places a very positive "spin" on performance improvement and uncovering blind spots.

o The professional management coach's job is not just to uncover blind spots, but also to motivate the manager to take part in a course of self-awareness that slowly erodes excessive defensiveness and promotes positive change. Coaches, by definition, are motivators. They are especially valuable when individuals have difficulty motivating themselves to engage in a self-assessment/self-improvement process.

Management coaching is a relatively new leadership training method. Highly interactive, dynamic training in human relations skills had previously employed "T-group" sessions and group-based sensitivity training. These methods emanated from change management theories and group training experiments pioneered by Kurt Lewin[12] and others.

The principles underlying these T-groups were sound, i.e., that managers need to understand how their behavior affects others and the dynamics of interpersonal communication. However, T-group and sensitivity training methods have been criticized for being too unstructured and for not building in the necessary on-the-job follow up, particularly for those who have undergone a particularly emotionally jarring T-group or sensitivity training experience. While these group-oriented human relations training methods are out of favor in some organizations, they can be beneficial when blended into a more comprehensive management development strategy that offers 1:1 management coaching thereafter. Such a combination of methods affords managers the opportunity to participate in powerful, dynamic group training experiences with the assurance that the self-awareness gained through them are integrated into a personalized, highly supportive leadership improvement plan.

360-Degree Appraisals

Blank's listing of traits of "natural born leaders" begins with those that fall under an opening section that encourages the reader to "Expand Self Awareness." In this section, Blank suggests that natural leaders are prone to "Seek 360-Degree Feedback;"[13]

> "They *(natural born leaders)* use all 360 degrees of input to evaluate performance. They want to know how their boss views their efforts. They rely on peers for feedback on ways to improve. They listen to those outside their organization for ideas. They seek out subordinates to gain valuable insights. They realize that others may have been in the same place they are now so they use their experience to help them move forward."[14]

Organizations formalize their leaders' need for this kind of comprehensive feedback by implementing a management development and/or performance review process called the 360-degree appraisal. The concept behind the 360-degree appraisal involves the value of obtaining subjective input on individual employees—most often those with management responsibilities—from multiple perspectives or sources. As Blank suggests, ratings should be gathered from supervisors, peers, customers and subordinates. In this way, managers receive feedback on how their performance is viewed by a number of organizational constituencies and stakeholders. This in turn leads to a more open, honest self-examination of one's strengths and potential blind spots. Managers then use this data as they structure a personal development plan that targets areas of management performance improvement that will require the most focus.

There are a wide variety of appraisal instruments from which to choose in performing a 360-degree feedback study on a particular manager or group of managers. The instrument used in soliciting the 360-degree appraisal must include issues related to the manager's <u>people skills</u>. There is considerable value in receiving subjective feedback on one's human relations competencies. The six essential management human relations practices we describe in this book all need to be addressed in the selected feedback tool.

Psychological Testing

While 360-degree feedback processes present subjective opinions to the manager about how he or she is perceived by others, psychological testing provides objective feedback based on an individual's responses to questions or statements that measure one's personality style and psychological type. With psychological testing, managers can learn about what a standardized, reliable, validated test instrument tells them, based on managers' own opinions about themselves.

Here are several psychological tests frequently administered in the workplace that are used to inform personnel decision-making and to assess an individual on a range of commonly-accepted leadership traits:

Myers Briggs Type Indicator® (MBTI®)

The Myers Briggs Type Indicator[15] is a self-report questionnaire designed to make Carl Jung's theory of "psychological type" understandable and useful in everyday life. The MBTI ® will help you identify your strengths and unique gifts. You can use the information to better understand yourself, especially in areas for potential growth.

"Psychological type" is a theory developed by Jung to explain apparently random differences in people's behavior. From his observations of clients and others, Jung found predictable and differing patterns of normal behavior. His theory of "psychological type" recognizes the existence of these patterns or types, and provides an explanation of how types develop.

According to Jung's theory, predicable differences in individuals are caused by differences in the way people prefer to use their minds. The core idea is that, when your mind is active, you are involved in one of two mental activities:

- Taking in information, or *perceiving*; or
- Organizing that information and coming to conclusions, or *judging*.

Jung observed that there are two opposite ways to perceive, which he called *sensing* and *intuition*, and two opposite ways to judge which he called *thinking* and *feeling*. Everyone uses these four essential processes daily in both the external world and the "inner world" we have been addressing in this chapter. Jung called the external world of people, things and experience *extroversion* and the internal world of inner processes and reflections *introversions*.

Jung believed that everyone has a natural preference for using one kind of *perceiving* and one kind of *judging*. He also observed that a person is drawn towards either the external world or the internal world more than the other. As you exercise your preferences, you develop distinct perspectives and approaches to life and human interaction.

The variations in what you prefer, use and develop lead to fundamental differences between people. The resulting predictable patterns of behavior form Psychological Type.[15]

Taking the Myers Briggs Type Indicator® can tell you a lot about how you interact with people, both at work and at home or in the community. It is a valuable self-assessment tool, and we encourage leaders to take it at least once to get a sense of what the MBTI ® tells you about your psychological tendencies.

California Psychological Inventory (CPI™)

The CPI™ assessment instrument[16] was developed years ago as a dynamic and objective measure of personality and behavior. The CPI™ provides an accurate, complex portrait of a client's professional and personal styles. It is a test developed specifically with the workplace and organizational leadership assessment in mind. The test provides a detailed personal portrait of an individual by describing personality characteristics across several scales, including a set of scales called "Folk Scales." The "Folk Scales" include an assessment of:

- Social expertise and interpersonal style (e.g., dominance, capacity for status, self-acceptance, empathy and others);
- Maturity, and normative orientation and values (e.g., responsibility, socialization, tolerance);
- Achievement orientation (e.g., achievement via conformance, achievement via independence); and
- Personal interest styles (e.g., psychological-mindedness, flexibility and femininity/masculinity).

In addition, thirteen "Special Purpose Scales" are available, to report on:

- Creative temperament
- Managerial potential
- Tough-mindedness
- A number of both practical and experimental dimensions of "operating style" and behavior.

As you can see, the CPI™ has a great deal of applicability to the kind of skills we are discussing in this book. We encourage managers to take this test prior to receiving individualized coaching. It helps them benchmark their strengths and limitations, as derived from a useful assessment tool specifically tailored to evaluating leadership qualities.[17]

Other assessment instruments that we have found useful in evaluating a client manager's tendencies include:

- *Thomas Kilman Conflict Mode Instrument*, which provides input specifically about one's style in managing conflict, as well as associated communication and personal effectiveness characteristics.
- *Fundamental Interpersonal Relations Orientation-Behavior™ (FIRO-B™)*, which is an instrument for those who want to understand individual personality dynamics, how personal needs affect interpersonal relationships and one's compatibility with others. Given our focus on interpersonal skills in the workplace, the FIRO-B™ is an inexpensive, easy-to-complete and quite valuable tool for managers to use as a means of expanding self-awareness in this area.[18]

You may self-administer all of these tests at various online psychological testing sites, for a modest fee (*see Appendix C*). Hopefully, we have whetted your appetite for learning as much as you can about yourself, your tendencies, how you perceive yourself and how you are perceived by others, all in the cause of developing leadership people skills. The basic premise is well-accepted: an awareness of your inner life and an openness to absorbing information from the world around you promote self-confidence, self-control and competent self-expression.

Ed Koch, former Mayor of New York City, was famous for walking the streets of the city and asking passers-by, "How am I doing?" This kind of openness to input from customers/constituents is, in essence, an openness to growth and positive change (not to mention that it also creates appreciation from those whose input is solicited). As you learn about yourself, you will begin making the right decisions about people. Sound judgments get noticed, particularly those about people, and this helps further your career and professional advancement within an organization.

Expanding self-awareness is a lifelong process. Its positive effects are cumulative. An avid interest in learning about ourselves actually makes it easier for us to be "other-oriented" and attuned to the unique circumstances of people around us. All efforts to examine ourselves are rewarded with the fruits of this labor: greater self-knowledge, self-possession, self-control and self-expression.

8

Following "Golden Rule" Principles

> *"To encourage the best work from the people we're responsible for, we need to consistently provide the kind of leadership we'd like to have for ourselves."*
> Janet Gallant, in "Simple Courtesies—How to Be a Kind Person in a Rude World"[1]

If there is a truly universal "rule" of human relationships, it can be summarized in the single succinct guideline promulgated by the ancient Jewish scholar Hillel in the first century A.D.: "Do not unto thy neighbor what is hateful unto thee; that is the whole law." The beauty of Hillel's insight lies in both the message itself and the message's inherent simplicity. Rephrased for the purpose of leadership development training, it tells managers, "Treat others the way you would like to be treated. That's really all you have to learn."

Indeed, it is a profound human revelation that so many religious and philosophical preaching about divinely-inspired human behavior revolve around this "Golden Rule." Consider some of the other variations on the Golden Rule theme from widely diverse societies and religions:

o *Christianity*: All things whatsoever ye would that men should do to you, do ye even so to them. *Matthew 7:12 and Luke 6:13.*

o *Buddhism*: Hurt not others in ways that you yourself would find hurtful—Udana-Varga, 5, 18.

o *Confucionism*: Surely it is the maxim of loving-kindness: Do not unto others that you would not have them do unto you. *Analects, 15,23.*

o *Brahminism*: This is the sum of duty: Do naught unto others which would cause you pain if done to you. *Mahabarata, 5, 1517.*

o *Islam*: No one of you is a believer until he desires for his brother that which he desires for himself. *Sunnah.*[2]

You may argue that the Golden Rule primarily applies to religion, to spiritual renewal sponsored by one's chosen faith. How does it apply to the rough-and-tumble world of secular business? Many organizations and the executives that lead them think it applies in a very fundamental way. J.C. Penney instituted the Golden Rule as the key operating tenet of the company. He was fond of saying, "The Golden Rule is still golden." Ewing Kauffman, a prominent executive in the pharmaceutical industry, insists that applying the Golden Rule to the management of his company makes eminent sense: "It's just good business practice," he insists. Mary Kay cosmetics champions its "golden rule management" code.[3]

If you agree that people skills matter a great deal in managing others, then the Golden Rule certainly figures prominently in formulating one's interpersonal communication style. It is the fundamental credo that supports how you communicate with others and how you make decisions that affect those around you.

What are the key aspects of following Golden Rule principles? How does virtually everyone want to be treated? Four core values stand out.

1. ***Treat people with respect.*** The amount of respect people bring to their interpersonal dealings with others is conveyed in many ways. The more obvious manifestations of respect include showing courtesy, being polite in interactions of all kinds. But as importantly, respect is also evidenced by a willingness to: listen attentively to others—*empathic listening is respectful!*; accept others' opinions and learn from them; delegate work; and share authority. Respect means refraining from condescension or acting superior.

   People have an intuitive feel for whether they are being treated with respect. There are many signals we send and receive that convey the level of respect being demonstrated. Good eye contact, extending a hand promptly in greeting, refraining from hurtful or insulting words or behaviors—these are all signs of respect for others that people appreciate.

2. ***Show fairness***, especially in decisions that affect other people. Doing what is right rather than what is expedient can be difficult, but it is widely admired. The Golden Rule's premise is that the best way to judge fairness is to turn the tables hypothetically. "How would I feel if I were in his, her or their place?" What would my reaction be if, to paraphrase one of Bob Dylan's songs, for just one day you could walk inside another person's shoes? Reflecting on the situation if the tables were turned adds valuable perspective. At times, it reinforces that a decision is correct. Managers have often shared with us that after they considered the Golden Rule implications of an action or statement, they proceeded with the decision nonetheless because it was inherently fair. But considering the other person's reactions as if

it were your own is a very valuable part of enlightened decision-making processes.

3. *Display honesty,* both in words and deeds. Nothing impugns a manager's reputation more than the "tag" of dishonesty. A manager's reputation for honesty can catapult his or her career, and a liar's tag is very harmful. People admire being leveled with. Conversely, it is insulting to be lied to. Lies contaminate human relations in ways that are difficult to repair. Trust builds at different speeds in people, but it deteriorates at a very rapid rate when it is betrayed.

   Honesty relates to the Golden Rule in obvious ways. Simply put, people expect others to be truthful to them, and are willing to be open and truthful to others in turn.

4. *Embrace diversity:* People in the modern workplace bring with them a range of different cultural and ethnic backgrounds. These differences should be cultivated for the valued perspectives they include. People are different, but people of different cultures all believe in the values inherent in the Golden Rule. Managers who lead diverse groups can turn the tables and ask themselves, "Even though I have a different background than some of those around me, I still expect that we can work together productively as long as:
   o   we see the value in others' unique cultural perspectives;
   o   we do not lose sight of the fact that we all have similar organizational goals;
   o   we all treat others as we expect to be treated—with respect, fairness, honesty and tolerance."

The Golden Rule gives us a consistent frame of reference, a model to follow when we are unsure about how to deal with people. As we apply this traditional principle, we gain a greater measure of control over our behavior and act in a more purposeful, caring and confident way. When we answer the question, "How would I like to be treated?" we also answer the question, "What should I do?"[3]

We have all been on the receiving end of rudeness and condescension, at work and away from work, and we know that these ways of speaking can make us feel hurt, angry and uncooperative. The Golden Rule moves us toward control of what we can control—our own actions and words. Managers that follow Golden Rule principles communicate more effectively because they become more consistent and less liable to take actions that they regret later. The Golden Rule permits us to think about the impact our words or actions might have on the listener or co-worker. It promotes perspective and disciplined behavior.

If managers follow Golden Rule principles, they behave in routinely admirable ways. Effective human relationships at work are built on the principle of mutual respect, backed up by fairness in decision-making and rigorously honest communications. People respond positively and productively to these demonstrations of personal characteristics in their leaders.

Treating others the way you would like to be treated is a management practice that is obvious in its merits but often overlooked in its application at work. Indeed, organizations need to reinforce respectful, fair and honest treatment of others consistently, in words and deeds. For managers invested in improving their people skills, being mindful of the Golden Rule is always useful. Following Golden Rule principles works synergistically with the other two blocks in the foundation layer of the management people skills pyramid. Practicing empathy means you care about what the other person is experiencing, you feel *with* them in part because you put yourself in their position and consider what it would be like for you—the essence of the Golden Rule. Expanding self-awareness helps you build an honest understanding of how you would like to be treated, and the value of fairness and personal respect. If you are able to tie these three practices together into a basic approach that guides the way you interact with people around you at work, your management human relations problems are likely to be few and far between.

9

Maintaining Proper Boundaries/Setting Appropriate Limits

"Being the leader of the Huns is often a lonely job."
From "Leadership Secrets of Attila the Hun," by Wess Roberts, Ph.D.

Introduction

How is it that leadership at the very top of a large organization can be a "lonely job?" In part, Attila the Hun's lament mirrors the feeling that compelled Harry Truman to place a famous sign on his Presidential desk:

"The buck stops here."

Leaders feel lonely because some decisions can't be shared with a peer or passed "up the ladder" to a higher position. Many final decisions rest on top leaders' shoulders and their shoulders alone. The gravity of these decisions may beg for outside assistance. However, individuals at the top rung of organizations do not have the advantage of access to peers or mentors that lower level decision-makers may use for support. After they collect all divergent input, leaders are frequently emotionally alone as they take responsibility for making ultimate choices that affect their organization's strategic direction.

The "loneliness at the top" paradigm is also a function of a top executive needing to avoid compromising interpersonal relationships with others in the organization. They recognize the importance of *maintaining appropriate personal boundaries with subordinates as a means of preserving a healthy position of authority.* Since every position in an organization reports up to the top executive, a feeling of solitude is understandable.

While these issues are very germane to CEOs, <u>all managers</u> experience situations when they need to assert their leadership role within their particular group. In this chapter, we will review proper leadership boundaries and how they contribute to a manager's ability to perform supervisory responsibilities equitably.

<u>Healthy Boundaries ≠ Remaining Distant and Disengaged</u>

The importance of personal boundaries that we discuss in this chapter do not preclude managers from remaining approachable, engaged and integrated with the groups they lead. With appropriate personal boundaries established, managers have a greater ability not only to exercise authority when they need to—which includes setting limits—but also to motivate their subordinates through empowerment, coaching and other actions that provide employee development opportunities. In discussing healthy supervisory boundaries, we are not advocating management isolation from or condescension to those under supervision. Indeed, it is a paradox of managerial practice that the strongest leaders are the least rigid and coercive with respect to directing their subordinates. Rather, strong leaders' focus is on achievement of organizational objectives.

Managing equitably: the influence of personal relationships

Part of the challenge of managing a group of people is making judgments that are perceived as fair. Fairness, as a key ingredient of Golden Rule principles, is a transcendent leadership quality. In more specific terms, though, it is important to emphasize one crucial aspect of leadership decision-making: *judgments cannot be influenced by non-work related factors.* Managers can't "play favorites." A major point of this Chapter is to emphasize how fairness and objectivity are seriously compromised when managers allow personal relationships with co-workers to interfere with their leadership authority.

Unambiguous Personal Boundaries

Let's begin by discussing examples of clear boundary violations for managers. These are situations when highly inappropriate interpersonal communication and/or relationships occur in the workplace. These situations do not require "judgment calls;" they are NEVER appropriate and must be avoided in all cases and at all times. When they do occur, the organization suffers not only from compromised managerial authority but also from bad publicity, public embarrassment, not to mention the risk of serious and costly litigation.

We hear about examples of workplace and leadership boundary violations all the time. Why? Because the fact is that they make news. People are titillated by the frailty of human judgment. We are fascinated when the top executive of a prestigious research university needs to resign after admitting to heavy drinking and other inappropriate social interactions with students. We read voraciously about a well-known and widely respected public administrator, discovered harassing a co-worker after an intimate relationship had been broken off by the co-worker, who appeared one evening uninvited at her home rifling through her personal belongings. We impeach a

President about dissembling testimony behind his scandalous affair with an intern less than half his age.

However, companies cope all the time with far less public controversies surrounding personal boundary violations by their supervisory staff. It is worth noting that the workplace is a microcosm for all human behavior. This includes behaviors that are self-destructive—or at the very least extremely imprudent. The fact is that "out-of-bounds" behaviors happen at the workplace and in many instances they occur within the leadership ranks. Unfortunately, it is the organization that bears much of the responsibility when these behaviors go unchecked.

Individuals in a position of management authority must avoid:

o   Romantic involvement with direct reports.
o   Exchanging remarks, emails or other communications with subordinates of an explicitly sexual nature, especially with employees of the opposite sex.
o   Exchanging remarks with subordinates that are culturally hateful and/or derogatory to different races, religions or cultural differences.
o   Indebtedness to a direct report.
o   Taking part in illegal or immoral activity or behavior with or around subordinates.

Romantic involvement with direct reports. Simply put, managing someone with whom you are romantically involved is NEVER acceptable. It is detrimental to the subordinate, to the organization and to the involved manager. It is a situation that is often kept concealed from team members, and maintaining this duplicity is no way to lead day in and day out. When the relationship is exposed, as it almost always seems to be, decisions that the manager makes become strongly colored by the fact that the romantic relationship exists. The risk of a sexual harassment lawsuit is enormous, placing both involved managers and organizations in jeopardy. Managers can heed the ethical standards of psychotherapists, which prohibit any romantic involvement with patients. The rationale is essentially the same for managers as it is for therapists: when proper boundaries are violated, all subsequent interactions are affected and the ability to be effective in one's professional role is compromised.

Exchanging remarks, emails or other communications with subordinates of an explicitly sexual nature, especially with employees of the opposite sex. The most egregious example of this behavior includes making improper sexual advances to a subordinate. However, it is also inappropriate to circulate profane jokes, pictures or messages under the guise of adding levity to the work environment. As with the ban against romantic involvement with staff members, this behavior places supervisors and organizations in serious legal jeopardy. The boundary/limit-setting issue noted here is not only problematic because of the legal risk involved. Subordinates who witness this type of sexually oriented communication by their supervisors come to feel that management condones such behavior. This can result in diminished discipline and respect within the group. Also, subordinates may experience disappointment or become mistrustful of the supervisors' judgment, which can compromise the supervisors' ability to lead.

Exchanging remarks with subordinates that are culturally hateful and/or derogatory to different races, religions or cultural differences. Using derogatory slang terms for an ethnic background or culture is NEVER acceptable behavior by a manager. Telling derogatory ethnic jokes is not appropriate in the workplace. The legal ramifications are severe, including the potential for employees to sue for civil rights discrimination protection. As importantly, managers with an interest in prioritizing human relations within their groups will have their efforts subverted by this type of communication behavior.

Indebtedness to a direct report. Managers who experience financial difficulties may look to family and friends for loans. A manager can NEVER solicit a loan or significant favor from someone who works under his or her supervision. This situation is unhealthy for a variety of reasons, not the least of which is the potential threats or coercion that could result if the loan or favor is not paid back promptly. A situation of indebtedness also creates emotional control by the loaner over the debtor, which subverts an indebted manager's ability to perform his or her organizational responsibilities.

Taking part in illegal or immoral activity or behavior with or around subordinates. This boundary violation concerns the importance of leading with integrity. Acting illegally or immorally not only subverts the organization's value system, it compromises authority. For example, if a manager were to use illegal drugs with subordinates at a party or social gathering, an unhealthy culture of secretiveness will often result within the organization. Similarly, if a subordinate becomes aware of his or her manager's marital infidelity, and is asked to cover up for the manager in exchanges with the manager's spouse, the ensuing interpersonal dynamics will alter the supervisory relationship considerably. Clearly, in placing a subordinate in such a moral dilemma, the manager is risking serious erosion of trust and loss of the means to motivate performance through espousal of shared values.

Maintaining Proper Boundaries

Most often, judgment is the key

While there is value in identifying "cut and dried" personal boundary violations that all managers must avoid, a parallel interest of this chapter involves helping managers build their judgment skills with respect to steering clear of conflicts of interest or interpersonal behavior that has the potential to erode one's ability to manage effectively. This judgment is a function of experience and awareness about the pitfalls of allowing personal relationships to compromise managerial authority. Learning about yourself and potential triggers of impulsive or self-destructive behaviors is also a key component of building judgment.

Physical contact is a good example of a potentially ambiguous boundary-related situation that may occur between a manager and his or her direct report. The physical boundary between two people working together in an organization is important to respect—especially when this physical touching is between people of different levels of authority and between members of the opposite sex. When we coach managers who present some difficulties in maintaining role-congruent physical boundaries with subordinates, we may ask these managers to provide their view on the distinctions and nuances of three examples of physical contact between people at work:

- A simple, short handshake;
- A light, encouraging tap on the back or an arm wrapped lightly around a subordinate's shoulder;
- Giving or receiving a neck massage.

Societal customs dictate the formality and respect for personal boundaries inherent in a business-like handshake. As such, handshakes are rarely inappropriate, even between different sexes. However, other touching behavior like a back slap or one-armed embrace gets more clouded and ambiguous. Between different sexes, such behavior moves into the "rarely appropriate" range. Some managers have a tougher time than others with seemingly innocuous, ostensibly healthy physical contact that they believe promotes positive human connection. We talk through different scenarios involving inter-gender physical contact, considering all the variables inherent in the diverse modern workforce. In the end, after all ramifications are evaluated, managers usually reach the conclusion that physical contact is probably not advisable, especially with individuals of the opposite sex. This is true even when there is a wide age discrepancy between the manager and the other person, or when the other person initiates the physical contact.

Once this insight is gained, the example of playfully giving a neck massage to someone else at work is a "no-brainer." If one needs to exercise caution about a back slap or a one-armed embrace around the shoulder, how could a neck massage ever be appropriate?

All in all, the legal and ethical realities of managing in the modern workplace require managers to be very discriminating about behavior that involves any physical contact with a subordinate. Touching is a very personal and potentially sexual behavior. People experience a wide range of reactions to touch, based on their personality, the degree and appropriateness of physical intimacy within their families and other causal factors. Managers never want to expose themselves to a touching incident that could be construed in any way as a sexual advance.

Here is another illustration of a judgment call that needs to be made, based on our list of unambiguous boundaries. Let's say a supervisor is asked to attend a retirement party at work, on company time, with no alcohol or other outside influences present. Attending this party would rarely be inappropriate, just as shaking a subordinate's hand is usually okay. Now let's say that the supervisor is also invited to attend a party given on the weekend by a subordinate. The supervisor decides not to attend, reasoning that he or she might be put in some type of compromising position, such as being witness to illicit drug use. Is the supervisor establishing healthy, if somewhat conservatively set boundary lines to maintain his or her proper authority at work? Or is his or her decision an over-reaction to an unreasonable fear? Avoiding the party could create the perception among co-workers that the manager is aloof and condescending, which has its own set of problematic ramifications. Where does the leader draw the line? Some leadership consultants advise top executives against attending any social gatherings with subordinates after work, claiming it is inadvisable ever to put oneself in a potentially compromising position. Others advise short, courteous stops at parties put on by subordinates, with a ready excuse to politely move on after a quick appearance. As managers move up the ranks, these kinds of decisions become more salient and often more difficult. Again, "being the leader of the Huns is often a lonely job."

Like a neck massage is an inadvisable example of physical touching in the workplace context, there are situations that are more overtly fraught with danger with respect to compromising one's leadership boundaries. A supervisor invited to share in a summer weekend beach house rental with a group of employees under his or her supervision needs to see how easily such a situation could lead to compromised authority and ambiguous supervisory relationships. Again, a manager would be hard pressed to find any rationale for accepting such an invitation, where personal and work boundaries are likely to be severely tested. This example, and countless others like it, require less "line-drawing" for supervisors. Mixing personal and professional closeness to this degree is just never a good idea.

The social nature of work

Throughout the day-to-day routines of the workplace, the social nature of work must be heeded and appreciated. Personal closeness, friendships and intimacy are common—even inevitable—results of people working together. After all, most people often spend as much if not more waking time in a workday with their workplace associates than they do with their family members.

Certainly, an involvement in teams and work groups often breeds personal closeness. When closeness creates bonds that build teamwork and mutual trust, the results for the organization can be very positive. Excellent managers know the importance that interpersonal respect and trust play in teamwork. They also understand the dangers that can occur when the boundary line between team members and team leaders is blurred. *The fact is that there is substantial overlap in the qualities of close relationships between team members and their team leaders that may help an organization under certain circumstances and may hinder an organization under different circumstances.*

Here is the criterion we advise in making judgment calls about how intimate a leader should become with his or her team:

> "Does my closeness with my team still allow me to manage (provide direction, set objectives, coach, counsel, appraise performance, etc.)? And do my team members understand and respect that I need to maintain the authority that comes with my supervisory position at all times?"

Setting Appropriate Limits

The correlation between maintaining boundaries and setting limits

Maintaining boundaries and setting limits within the group that a manager leads are very related concepts. When a manager's role and authority are clear, his or her ability to set limits is enhanced. Without the requisite role boundary in place, the manager's ability to say "no" or establish performance standards can be seriously compromised. These situations do not go unnoticed by higher levels of management, who expect their supervisors to be remain in control of their assigned groups.

Let's review a case example when management limit-setting diminished as a result of ambiguous personal boundaries.

> Tim Smith has been promoted to supervisor of an area with which he has had little previous operational experience. One of his new direct reports, Tina Ciotti, has much more

experience in the area Tim is now supervising. Tim has known Tina for many years. In fact, Tina is his wife's best friend, and his daughter's godmother. Needless to say, they socialize frequently outside work.

Given Tina's experience and his relative inexperience in the new area he is supervising, Tim looks to Tina for guidance about many decisions that have to be made. This occurs so often that Tina begins making decisions on her own and then informs Tim of them after the fact. Her feeling is that she is being asked what to do anyway, so she decides to save time and act on her own judgment.

Inevitably, Tim is caught unaware of one of these decisions that Tina makes. Before he learns about one of Tina's decisions, Tim's supervisor approaches him and asks about the rationale for a change in procedure that his area has just instituted on its own accord. He is told that other departments are complaining about it. When Tim has to beg ignorance of the situation, he is scolded for his lax supervision of Tina and his area.

In this case example, the manager's problem stemmed in part from his allowing an implicit reversal of roles to take place between himself and a respected, competent direct report. Limits were not set, the line of authority became unclear, the boundaries became blurred. Tim's friendship with Tina outside of work may have contributed to his unwillingness to reinforce the expectation that all decisions were ultimately his to make. Further, the friendship outside work may have led Tina to assume that she did not need to follow customary subordinate-manager communication procedures. She may have assumed their personal bond was such that he would trust her to make decisions because she had his interests in mind when she made the decisions.

While Tina's usurping of Tim's management role may have been inno-
cent enough and driven by good intentions, the end result was criticism
of Tim's performance by his supervisor. Here are some points to consider in assessing the boundary issues in this case example, including
how such a circumstance might have been avoided and how it could be
corrected:

- From the beginning of his supervisory assignment, how might Tim
  have asserted his authority and control in his new area while also
  tapping into Tina's experience with the area's operations?
- If the events occurred as described, how might Tim approach Tina
  to regain authority of his new area? What problems might Tim
  experience in confronting Tina about this incident?
- How will their friendship outside work affect this discussion?

Common boundary-related challenges for managers

Managers are constantly faced with instances when they must make
decisions, communicate directions and correct performance flaws that
may leave some subordinates disappointed or in a state of disagreement. Doing the right thing for the organization does not always dove-
tail with the interests of a particular person under a manager's
supervision. A manager's personal relationship with those under his or
her supervision is an important variable in terms of maintaining an
ability to make the right decisions even when they may disappoint or
anger a particular team member.

Below, two common and potentially troublesome situations are discussed related to a supervisor's personal relationship with his or her
subordinates. They both have to do with managers' ability to maintain
boundaries and set limits in situations that test the issue of how personal relationships affect leadership responsibilities. These include:

Assuming supervisory responsibility and authority over former peers/co-workers.

Moving into a supervisory position over a former peer or group of peers tests an individual's human relations skills. The objective is to make an effective transition from the role of co-worker to that of being "the boss." Ideally, there will be considerable communication and a "working through" of the situation in which a previous peer relationship morphs into a supervisor/subordinate relationship. Discussion and agreement between the new boss and former co-workers about the implications—both at work and away from work—can lead to an agreement about what aspects of the former relationship need to change and what aspects can remain "as is." A supervisor needs to be empathic about the emotional effect that such a transition will have on the former co-worker. A positive and reinforcing message needs to be sent to the former co-worker(s) that while things may be different in some respects, there are advantages to the new situation as well. These advantages may include the trust and open channel of communication that exists in the relationship already (as opposed to a situation where an unknown individual might have received the position).

An individual's behavior—both on and off the job—needs to be different when he or she is promoted to a leadership role over former peers than it was previously. How different is a matter of good judgment and prudent behavior at work. Certainly the promoted former co-worker needs to take heed of all the unambiguous boundary violations described previously. But the supervisor can also expect that many more situations will occur that are essentially in a "gray area"—where judgments about maintaining boundaries are less clear cut. Often, the new boundaries of the supervisor/subordinate relationship will be tested early. This limit-testing behavior is aimed at determining how the supervisor intends to establish his or her leadership role and newly granted authority over former co-workers. The awareness that the role will be tested helps the new manager prepare a response that establishes a firm boundary while minimizing the former co-workers' emotional hurt and resentment.

Managing familial relatives or other persons with whom the manager has had a highly intimate personal relationship.

Is this ever a good idea? In most cases, no—it is not. It is simply too difficult to maintain proper supervisory boundaries with a relative or close personal friend/ex-friend. Only in rare cases do such situations work. However, there may be times when business requirements dictate that such an arrangement be allowed for a short period of time, until alternative arrangements can be made. A healthy discussion about boundary expectations and the impact of the arrangement on others within the work group will help establish some "rules" for the special arrangement. Labeling the arrangement "interim" or temporary creates the latitude to revert to other options once these alternatives become available.

Some Final Thoughts

Turning around a lax, undisciplined atmosphere that developed either under one's own or another manager's command

In some work environments, a lax, undisciplined atmosphere can develop. Employees arrive to work late, leave work early, take extended breaks, take advantage of company resources for personal use, etc. As we have discussed, there is a strong correlation between lax management and a situation where a manager's boundaries are unclear or have been compromised. It is difficult to make subordinates accountable when they do not respect the authority of their supervisors.

There are a couple of ways to resolve this organizational problem. One, of course, is to put a new manager in charge who is able to establish boundaries and set limits. A fresh approach is often best for effecting needed change.

Another is to employ organizational leadership development resources to train/coach the existing manager to rehabilitate his or her authority. This rehabilitation must begin with the manager taking specific measures to reinforce proper roles and boundaries. This includes delineating—usually in both verbal and written form—performance expectations, limits that need to be clarified and work accountabilities. Then, the manager needs to follow through on these freshly communicated expectations. Supervisory behaviors will need to be consistent and equitable.

This rehabilitation takes considerable effort and mental energy. The manager's willingness to follow through on setting prescribed limits will be continuously tested, especially by those who preferred the lax environment. But managers who communicate effectively and remain vigilant about maintaining performance expectation boundaries can turn around a previously dysfunctional and/or undisciplined group.

A word on the issue of supervisory boundaries and advocacy for "boundarylessness" in organizations:

Some eminent experts in organizational behavior and theory—including General Electric's former CEO Jack Welch—advocate for a "boundaryless" organization.[1] Is this view contrary to the points we are making in this chapter? The answer is—not at all. An advocacy for boundarylessness in an organization emphasizes the value of eliminating "turf battles" and power struggles between individuals and departments. These conflicts detract from an organization's ability to achieve its mission. Leadership experts wish to avoid the establishment of "fiefdoms" within an organization: departments or divisions that operate independently and are focused on sustaining a power base rather than working flexibly with others in advancing the health and performance of the overall organizational entity.

Our emphasis is not on cross-functional boundaries but on the personal boundaries between employees and the individuals that are managing their work. Here is an example of the point we are making: Jack Welch has written that he would rejoice when a subordinate manager decides not to stay late at work trying to predict what Mr. Welch may ask him in a project meeting the following day. In response to a question to which this manager did not know the answer, Mr. Welch would rather have this individual answer, "I don't know, but I'll find out and let you know as soon as possible." Mr. Welch would be pleased that the manager's response wasn't affected by the rank of the person asking the question, and that the team goal of understanding the answer to the question was the focus rather than appearances.

We have no doubt, though, that Mr. Welch would not want his managers to lead or behave in a way that made their managerial authority ambiguous or compromised. He would expect managers to exercise good judgment about not allowing personal relationships with subordinates mitigate their ability to rate performance, establish accountability or make personnel decisions.

Maintaining appropriate boundaries as a "people skill"

The essential skill being discussed in this Chapter is *judgment*, judgment about human relations at work. It is a skill that requires an understanding about the dynamics of workplace supervision and about how productive, authority-maintaining supervisory relationships are developed between people. It involves mediating impulses that, if not checked or delayed, will lead managers into inappropriate behaviors that get them into trouble.

Setting limits and a Theory Y management style

A superficial comparison of Theory Y management approaches and the concept of supervisory limit-setting may seem contradictory. With Theory Y's emphasis on trusting the inherent traits within their staff to work hard, take initiative and grow as individuals, boundary issues and limit-setting may seem a bit out of context. Earlier in the chapter we addressed the issue of how establishing boundaries is not equivalent to being distant or disengaged from staff members. But an additional point needs to be made. The fact is that Theory Y managers establish their leadership authority from the basis of an empowering and trusting supervisory approach. This approach is a means toward a valued, positive outcome: namely, higher levels of productivity, morale and teamwork. Theory Y and *SOLID people management* competencies do not erode authority, they reinforce it. Individuals respect their leaders who motivate them to do the best they can, and this respect is a key ingredient in establishing a leader's authority.

10

Criticizing Artfully

> "*...used artfully, feedback on competencies can be a priceless tool for self-examination—and for cultivating change and growth. Used poorly, it can be an emotional bludgeon.*"[1]
>
> Daniel Goleman, Ph.D., in his book "Working with Emotional Intelligence"

Introduction

Most managers prefer "the carrot" to "the stick" in supervising work performance. Motivating employees by means of positive reinforcement is usually far less of a managerial challenge than having to criticize or, in worse case scenarios, having to take disciplinary action for errors, omissions or other sub-par work performance. Yet few managers escape the requirement to address situations when criticism of a subordinate is warranted and a necessary part of maintaining a productive workforce.[2]

The managerial challenge in criticizing an employee's performance is part internal and part external. The internal challenge involves gathering the mental courage to confront a subordinate with the performance problem. Courage is needed because of the external part of the challenge: the other person's typical defensive and emotional reaction to the criticism.

Let's face it—it is not easy being on the receiving end of an encounter in which the message is that performance is poor or that an avoidable mistake has been made. In addition to making a person feel defensive, the entire process of being criticized can be hurtful and discouraging. Depending on the criticized person's personality and what psychologists call his or her "ego strength"—the innate sense of oneself, or self-worth—the encounter is likely to make the criticized person feel angry, anxious, depressed or all of the above. We refer to this as the "emotional fallout" of criticism that managers can control with superior "people skills."

Counterproductive, even pathological behavior of disgruntled employees whose work has been criticized can manifest itself. For example, the behavior may include:

- Withdrawing from a group or team, or become uncommunicative with the criticizing supervisor;
- "Acting out," or engage in attention-getting behavior, intended to exact some direct or indirect retribution for the critical remarks;
- Acting "passive-aggressively," or trying to be hurtful to the manager or overall organization through inaction or inertia;
- Feeling insecure and less decisive, bringing other departments to a standstill;
- Manifesting inappropriate anger that creates more frequent disagreements and conflicts;
- Engaging in "splitting," or trying to create factions for and against the supervisor;

- Becoming demoralized about working for the company, because of disappointment in the overall organization for sanctioning the criticism;
- Resigning from the organization. This is a costly result of an incident of performance criticism, particularly when the chastised employee is valuable in many ways and resignation is avoidable.

Our present discussion focuses most on means to <u>prevent these behaviors when they are avoidable</u>, by framing criticism in ways that create the best opportunity for a productive ongoing supervisory relationship.

How can criticism be "artful"?

By definition, "artful" managerial behavior entails *considered, creative responses* to difficult interpersonal situations involving the supervision of someone else's work. To be "more art than science," managerial criticism needs to involve:

- Building an experienced view of how interpersonal communication can be molded to particular circumstances.
- Balancing the importance of the message being delivered, i.e., that the performance needs improvement, with the importance of delivering it in a way that does not undermine the feedback but rather encourages its acceptance and creates motivation for the desired performance improvement.
- Resisting rash, impulsive, demeaning attacks. An artful approach is thoughtful, not reactive.
- Expanding one's personal skills for motivating human behavior, and approaching management tasks with empathy.

Indeed, an artful, creative approach to workplace communication considers ways to understand and respond to the unique circumstances of the other person—the definition of empathy—and how to best use insights gleaned from empathic exchanges in order to achieve the desired supervisory objectives.

Avoiding Criticism "In the Heat of the Moment"

Most employers have policies and procedures that include regular, scheduled meetings to conduct performance evaluations where corrective input can be shared. It is easier for the manager to prepare him or herself to provide corrective input and expectations in these prescribed meetings whose function is mutually understood by both supervisor and direct report.

Table 10-1 lists some guidelines for preparing for pre-scheduled, formal performance reviews where "bad news" needs to be delivered in order to turn around inadequate job performance.

Table 10-1

Preparing for Performance Reviews: Delivering the Message About
the Need for Work Improvement

- *Have documentation available*
- *Make sure you have documented the times you have spoken to the employee about his/her performance*
- *Have written quality standards to show to the employee*
- *Show the employee examples of how his/her work does not meet standards as well as the work of others*
- *Have a list prepared of changes you would like the employee to make in his/her performance*
- *Be positive about the employee's ability to improve*
- *Set short term goals for the employee*
- *Be honest about the employee's future, without being patronizing or admonishing*
- *Develop a mutually agreed-to contract to improve performance within a set amount of time*

From "Productive Performance Appraisals" by Randi T. Sachs[3]

However, much criticism of job performance is reactive; there exists an urgency to address a specific performance error or flaw, so that it is not repeated. Organizational stressors—time constraints, deadlines, pressures from other departments affiliated with the project and other factors—can play a major part of the context in which criticism is delivered. When high levels of work stress or pressures combine with a need to criticize the work of a subordinate it may be difficult to do so in an artful, considered and creative way. It is important for managers to remain aware of this fact, and develop more engrained communication skills so that interactions that occur in "the heat of the moment" do not differ widely from more controlled, planned performance discussions.

One key to artful criticism is the ability to gain a sense of *perspective*, or an ability to keep ultimate objectives in mind. Maintaining perspective breeds self-control, and curbs over-reactions when things go off course. *The artful critic never "shoots from the lip;"* he or she is able to keep an employee's development, sense of self-worth, morale and team spirit in mind despite the external pressures that can build up and "push buttons" that are better off unplugged or disabled.

Let's create a case example to demonstrate how stress can impact the emotional aspects of criticizing a subordinate's behavior. We will then stay with this case example as we go on to discuss practical techniques of artful criticism.

Case Example

An engineering firm's senior marketing executive, Ms. Thurmond, supervises the work of a marketing manager, Ms. Jones. Ms. Jones hands a finished Proposal to Ms. Thurmond to review before it is to be submitted to a prospective client. In reviewing the Proposal, Ms. Thurmond finds pages out of order, and in several spots the numbers do not add up. Ms. Thurmond will have to meet with Ms. Jones and note the mistakes so that the Proposal can be corrected and reviewed again before being sent out.

Consider the effect of situational stress: What impact would it have on this meeting if Ms. Thurmond had two other pressing work commitments that day, and the Proposal was due to the client by mid-afternoon the next day? What if the Proposal wasn't due for another two weeks?

The Sandwich Technique

Conveying bad news is an unpleasant task. But there are valuable, widely used strategies for doing so diplomatically and tactfully. One of the most common and effective of these involves "sandwiching" the bad news between positive or upbeat statements. If you incorporate this fundamental technique into your managerial repertoire, you are bound to be more effective at delivering corrective criticism to those under your supervision. It will also add to your overall skills in diplomacy and tact, which are admired traits of leaders—particularly at higher levels of an organization.

The "Sandwich Technique" requires that:

- One NEVER opens an interaction with a criticism or negative statement. The opening must ALWAYS be positive.

- The criticism or corrective feedback is then shared, but this should NEVER be the final statement.

- The final statement must ALWAYS BE POSITIVE AND AFFIRM-ING. In this way, the recipient of the news or feedback is cushioned to the emotional reaction of the criticism both before it is communicated and after it is communicated.

This technique is so broadly used that it becomes second nature to any function that must convey bad news or offer critical feedback. Think about letters or messages that recruiters deliver to job applicants when a position will not be offered. They will usually begin with statements about how the interviewers liked the applicant very much, saw much strength in the candidacy, and this made the selection very difficult. Then the bad news is conveyed—the company has selected another, more highly qualified candidate. The communication will then end with a statement wishing the applicant good luck in their obviously promising future.

The same kind of strategy of layering the message of criticism between positive, affirming introductory and closing statements should serve as a core framework for managers engaging in performance criticism. Again, the rule is NEVER to begin to address a mistake or performance problem with a critical remark. The opening statement is ALWAYS positive about the person. It could be a comment on the good job they did on another recent project, how well they handled a recent situation, etc. It can also be a general statement about the employee's value to the team. In considering how to perform a performance criticism using the Sandwich Technique, you will need to be prepared to open with an aspect of an employee's work performance that you both feel is going well. At times this may take some creativity, but there is ALWAYS something positive that a manager can say about an employee's capabilities.

In our case example of the hypothetical senior marketing executive who found numerous errors in a Final Proposal she was asked to review, her positive statement might be something like:

> *"Preparing this Proposal obviously involved a lot of good hard work."*

Then the performance issue is raised.

> *"I do need to understand, though, how the Proposal ended up with all the errors it had in it when it was given to me for final review. Walk me through who was part of the process of writing, compiling and editing this Proposal, and how much time you spent in organizing and reviewing it."*

This leads to a discussion of the performance problem and ways to correct it in the future. Before closing the discussion, a positive affirming "stroke" should be shared.

> *"This discussion was extremely helpful. Your ideas and judgment are very good. It sounds like we are on the same page. I'm feeling quite confident that you can implement what we decided, and that this problem won't recur."*

In raising the concern you have about a specific incident, mistake or performance flaw, consider these fundamental techniques:[4]

* *Get the facts straight*: Benjamin Disraeli once said that it is much easier to be critical than to be correct. Make a sincere effort to be correct. Having available all appropriate documentation can be especially helpful in assembling and verifying factual information.

* *Choose the best timing*: Criticizing performance promptly—say, within 48 hours of a problem which if left uncorrected will continue to fester and have negative implications for the team or overall organization's productivity—is often advisable when there is an urgency to make corrections. The danger, again, is in allowing situational stress affect how you deliver the message in the "heat of the moment." In our case example, the best immediate action might be to focus on what needs to get done to get the Proposal out to the client expeditiously, i.e., identifying the mistakes, making the corrections, proofreading and getting it prepared for mailing. This avoids a situation in which strong emotional fallout from the criticism affects the completion of a time-constrained work objective—in this case, getting the Proposal to the client on time. The meeting

to discuss the Proposal's poor quality can be set up at some time later, i.e., after the stress has diminished.

Another time to have the critical interaction is just before there is an opportunity for the employee to repeat the mistake. In our previous case example, Ms. Thurmond might meet with the Ms. Jones several days before another significant Proposal is due to address the previous Proposal's problems, so that the Proposal she is about to receive does not have the same kind of mistakes.

- *Avoid criticizing "in public"*: The emotional fallout of being critical will increase exponentially if you do not have the self-control or perspective to avoid belittling someone in front of others. Doing so is just never a good practice. Besides, the techniques we encourage take time to employ, and it is wasteful of other people's time to be party to the discussion.

- *Control the setting:* Ideally, criticism should be delivered in a meeting behind closed doors. This helps create a setting for a private, open discussion that is not affected by external stimuli or interruptions.

- *Condemn the deed, not the doer:* Hate the sin, not the sinner. Reject the performance, not the performer. In our case example, Ms. Thurmond might express her concern by noting,

"The Proposal was not nearly ready to be sent out. I'm concerned about our quality assurance process if a the final draft of a Proposal gets to me with this number of errors."

This de-personalization of the criticism places the focus on the flawed Proposal and the review process, not on Ms. Jones herself.

- *Use "you" sparingly:* As above, in focusing on the errors rather than the person, managers avoid excessive defensiveness that can impede progress toward problem resolution. Consciously avoiding the word "you" during the criticism segment of the Sandwich Technique helps keep emotionally-laden blaming out of the conversation.

  Consider the difference in the emotional reaction one is likely to experience in response to each of the following two statements:

  Negative, blaming statement: "How could you hand me this Proposal to review when there are so many obvious errors in it?"

  More appropriate: "We have to talk about how this Proposal made it me for final review with so many obvious mistakes still in it."

  When using the word "you" or "your", it is best intertwined with help-seeking statements, such as, "Give me your sense of…" or "Help me understand how involved you were at different stages of the Proposal editing."

- *Probe empathically with open-ended questions:* Listen actively to the employee as he or she describes issues surrounding the performance problem. Make an effort to probe for what is being left unsaid. For example, Ms. Thurmond might reflect the feeling in Ms. Jones' explanations that she sounds very stressed and may be resentful about being "stretched too thin."

- *Don't change the subject or allow the subject to be changed. Select key issues and restrict yourselves to them:* Stay on task, and confront attempts to move the discussion to other topics. Refrain from far-reaching discussions with countless variables. Prepare a mental or written list of the issues that need to be addressed.

After wrapping up the performance correction meeting with a positive statement, it is often best to discontinue any further discussion of other side issues so that the impact of the encounter can sink in.

The Importance of Follow Up

Obviously, a great way to mitigate the sting of criticism is to look for an opportunity to review how well the employee has heeded the message about performance improvement, and then be generous with praise for work well done the next time a similar task is completed competently. Looking for chances to provide praise should receive far more effort than continuing to seek out inadequacies or things to criticize about a subordinate's work. This is especially true when the emotional fallout of criticism is more profound.

However, if the problem persists, you may need to recycle the criticism process with more urgency and seriousness. The positive components may need to be tempered by additional concern that the positives are becoming harder to identify, i.e., the well of tolerance for mistakes is running dry.

Advanced Artful Criticism

The Sandwich Technique and the guidelines for delivering criticism discussed so far are engrained in fundamentals of effectively managing other people. Now, let's look at some aspects of the process of criticizing the work of someone under your supervision that raises the level of the "art" to a higher plane. These are more advanced techniques or skills because they involve a higher degree of empathy, a strong investment in being attuned to the feelings of others and a seasoned "big picture" perspective about what is really important in leadership.

- *Don't expect to eliminate defensiveness entirely*: It is naïve to think that the person receiving criticism will not have a negative "knee-jerk" reaction to it at first. Managers should focus less on the common initial reaction that is bound to be more of an emotional reaction to criticism, and focus more on the secondary response, i.e., the behavior in the days or weeks that follow. When the message of support and affirmation that concludes the properly conducted performance correction discussion is heeded, and the sting of criticism wears away, the secondary response may "kick in" with evidence of positive changes and improved work output.

- *An empathic communicator will reflect the feeling in the interaction*: Defensiveness and discouragement should be noted if evident. After feelings are reflected, the artful criticism continues with a message that this discussion is not about the employee but the employee's performance. The focus is not on the negative but on how to fix the problem so that positive things can happen in the future.

- *Examine your heart*: Before beginning interactions in which you will need to criticize a subordinate, ask yourself (or even better, discuss openly with a supportive mentor or coach) how you are feeling about this situation. Are you angry? Do you feel betrayed in some way? Do you feel a need for retribution or to get even for something that occurred in the past? If so, your approach is likely to be emotionally charged. It is likely to come across as an attack, as punitive. The emotionally intelligent manager develops more natural introspection skills, and a willingness to acknowledge how feelings affect behavior.

- *Defuse anxiety and defensiveness with humor and creativity*: Humor is a great icebreaker and stress reducer, and self-deprecating humor can humanize you in your subordinate's eyes. A humorous, lighter touch requires substantial creativity and a good delivery. But when effective, it can be very effective at minimizing defensiveness while getting the point across. Attempts at humor can lighten the moment, and draw a smile from the employee being criticized. This can shift the tone of the interaction to one that is less contentious and stressful.

- *Be calm and firm in coping with inappropriate emotional or behavioral reactions to the criticism.* As we noted in the Introduction, one of the difficult aspects of criticizing work performance is handling the emotional fallout of the critical encounter. At times, this emotional fallout can be severe and very disturbing. The behavior may include:

  o *Excessive tearfulness*: An emotionally fragile employee may cry uncontrollably after being criticized. This can make a manager feel very guilty and cruel.
  o *Excessive anger, manifested by shouting, screaming, use of profanity*: Some employees lose control by flying into a rage, raising their voice and using profanity that is inappropriate in the work setting. This can create a range of emotions in managers that witness this behavior, including fear, anxiety, and reactive anger on part of the managers themselves.
  o *Inappropriate avoidant behavior*. These may include walking out before the discussion is formally ended, or "clamming up" and refusing to speak;
  o *At an extreme, threats of violence or intimidation*: We have all become much more attuned to real-life incidents of workplace violence. The threat posed by disgruntled employees who act out their rage violently may be very real. Often, these violent

employees have been terminated or had their work strongly criticized.

Here are some tips for handling these uncomfortable situations:

a) **Ensure privacy to minimize the employee's embarrassment.** If the door or window shades are open to the office or room where you are meeting, get up and close/draw them if the employee's emotions are escalating. The decrease in stimulation can help create a better setting for defusing the situation.

b) **Remain calm.** Don't become agitated yourself by an outpouring of emotion. Try not to appear frightened of excessive emotional behavior, unless actual threats or intimidating remarks are made. In those cases, a healthy fear of the employee may be indicated, and may warrant summoning security or other people to join the meeting.

c) **Maintain an even, soothing, calm but firm voice.** If possible and credible, provide reassurances and positive statements to try to raise the employee's immediate self-esteem. Never answer shouting with more shouting.

d) **Exercise empathy.** Affirm your feeling that this is a difficult situation for the both of you.

e) **Offer compassion.** Keep a box of tissues available for tearful reactions.

f) **Insert a self-deprecatory or humorous remark to lighten the mood.** In our case example, if the criticized employee becomes extremely tearful, the senior marketing executive might say in a lighthearted, "tongue-in-cheek" manner as she offers a box of tissues,

"Now don't use all of those tissues, I may need some of them if we don't win this bid."

Part of the artfulness of this attempt at humor is that it refocuses the discussion on the ultimate objective, i.e., winning the business.

g) **Offer a "time-out".** Allow the criticized employee to calm him/herself down. You can excuse yourself to use the bathroom or to run a quick errand, and note that this will give the employee a few minutes to get composed. When appropriate, make a decision to reconvene the meeting later, when the employee has regained his/her self-control.

h) **Don't try to restrain an employee who gets up to leave or actually leaves a meeting before you feel the discussion is over.** Ask the employee who makes a move to bolt from your performance correction meeting to stay until the two of you have a full understanding of the issues and the resolution plan. Do so very politely but firmly. If he/she doesn't listen, don't force the issue. While trying to talk the person into staying to finish the meeting is appropriate, don't "bar the door" or physically prevent an agitated employee from leaving the office or room.

For employees who "clam up," use empathic statements about what you are observing and feeling from the employee's refusal to speak or discuss the situation. Allow some silence to occur. Sometimes the employee might be more uncomfortable with silence than you are, and begin speaking again. If the refusal to speak continues, re-state the key messages and consequences, emphasize that your "door is always open" to discuss this further, and terminate the meeting.

The Results of Artful Criticism

Managers who handle incidents well when a subordinate's work requires criticism examine their own motivations, and have a handle on their feelings and affective reactions to what has occurred. This helps them expand their self-awareness which improves all aspects of their management human relations practices. These managers develop engrained diplomatic and tactful ways of addressing problems, so that criticisms are never antagonistic, insulting, attacking or punitive. They develop a way to use humor appropriately to get their point across and mitigate the sting of critical feedback.

How do managers know if they are successfully developing these "people skills"? In part, it is in observing the positive results that follow. Subordinates make fewer mistakes, correct performance problems and do so without "acting out" or engaging in other negative behaviors to exact retribution for the criticism. Addressing a performance issue should lead not only to improved work, but to a higher level of trust in the managers' competency and willingness to address future problems in a similarly constructive way.

11

"Flexing" To Different People Styles

> "One person thought about results; the other thought about process. They saw the world through totally different frames of reference. Neither understood how the other thought or operated—each stressed out by the other. Sound familiar?"
> Ron Willingham in "The People Principle"[1]

Introduction

Before we begin explaining the capstone building block in our management people skills pyramid, *flexing to different people styles*, let's return to the base of our *SOLID Pyramid* model for a moment. In Chapter 6, we explained how managers *practicing empathy* approach workplace interactions with an interest in understanding and responding to the unique circumstances of the people around them. Chapter 7 described how leaders grow by developing useful insights about their emotional "inner self," their personality and leadership style. This awareness about oneself contributes to burgeoning self-confidence, greater self-control and competent self-expression.

Clearly, these two fundamental skills, practicing empathy and expanding self-awareness, are highly inter-related. "Reading" other people, a feature of empathetic individuals, involves skills that correlate directly with an ability to identify and label one's own emotions. Further, the empathic, self-aware individual knows how he or she would like to be treated, thus making it easier to apply Golden Rule principles.

Empathy and self-awareness contribute to an interpersonal style that is apt to look for layers of meaning in the words and behaviors of others. While some workplace communication can be taken at face value, the nature of human interactions is that it is often complex and multi-dimensional. Effective communicators engage other people by probing for issues, ideas and feelings that lie beneath the surface. They look beyond what is said and try to discover what is left unsaid. Empathic, self-aware individuals also focus on *who* is saying what is being said, *how* things are said, the *context* within which it is said and, when relevant, they can make educated assumptions about *why* it was said *in the way* it was said.

Deeper understandings about people stem from an ability to observe behavior in a non-judgmental way. Theory Y managers have an abiding curiosity about what motivates and drives people. They are intrigued by the nature of stylistic differences between individuals. They have seen a payoff when they nurture more intrinsic rewards for good job performance that are specific to particular types of individuals. They analyze peoples' interpersonal communication styles as a way to develop a strategy for building relationships with these individuals. They do so even when these personal styles are quite different from their own.

This chapter will emphasize the value of managers' adapting their approach to others, as a means of developing more productive, "people-oriented" supervisory rapport. We will describe the common motivations and personalities that employees manifest at work. We will outline how managers' ability to read people, engage them creatively through a positive assessment of their intents and motivations, then "flex" to their innate "people styles" improves the potential that their relationships with those under their supervision will be positive and productive.

Flexibility in relating to others is certainly characteristic of executive leadership. As executives move up the corporate ladder and take on new, additional responsibilities, they usually assume leadership of more departments or more divisions. Managing more departments or divisions means managing a greater total number of employees. An executive with more aggregate numbers of staff to manage is very likely to encounter different styles of people under his or her authority. Effective executives understand that it is not easy to change people, but one can adapt one's own behavior to get the most out of a work relationship with those who present different personalities and approaches to problem-solving.

In our view, an interest in finding deeper understandings within human communication and behavior is invaluable to the process of developing a potent, natural people leadership style with limitless possibilities for personal and professional growth. This is particularly true in the context of problem-solving and managing conflicts. In these situations, the manager skilled in human relations will begin by trying to "identify positive intent."

By "positive intent," we mean the good purpose meant to be served by a particular communication or behavior.[2] We have found it useful to approach communications with others by assuming that all behavior originates from this "positive intent." Such an approach is infinitely more conducive to producing healthy discussion and fruitful dialogue, while mitigating the resentments that result inevitably from more negative, angry and blaming forms of communication. In essence, looking for positive intent is a way to avoid "shooting from the lip," a behavior that we denounced in the previous Chapter on artful criticism. It helps individuals consider meanings behind behavior, rather than just reacting to the behavior itself. It promotes a longer-term perspective on problem assessment and problem resolution.

This approach is neither naïve nor overly optimistic. It does not turn managers into "Polyannas" who see no malevolent agendas in human behavior. Certainly, quite negative behaviors occur in workplaces, there is no doubt about that. But even blatantly negative behaviors can be perceived and understood as originating in some positive intent. Making the effort to find this positive intent exercises a manager's people skills and perceptiveness about human behavior. It assumes a need not only to solve problems but also to maintain relationships with the other people that can be productive and motivating going forward.

Needs drive behaviors and their intent

Before discussing specifics about identifying positive intent as one manages others, it is helpful to understand the "hierarchy of needs"[3] that people experience at work. Positive intents are driven by the needs one experiences on the job. These needs evolve and migrate between levels based on experience, seasoning, time spent on a position, business success and the leadership style of senior management.

The "lowest common denominator" of work motivation is based on the need to feel safe, both physically and emotionally. The threats one experiences on the job can range from unsafe working conditions in certain jobs to insecure working conditions in other jobs. For example, employees may feel emotionally insecure and financially unsafe if they work in an industry that is undergoing large layoffs and widespread reductions in force.

Assuming the individual feels safe, both physiologically and occupationally, the next level of need may "kick in." This level involves more social needs: the need to belong, to associate with others or peers, to gain acceptance by others, to develop friendships.

Next, one progresses to needs related more to one's ego and professional identity. Here, employees seek work that builds self-confidence, fosters independence and/or helps gain status and recognition.

Finally, one can look to one's job for self-actualization and self-fulfillment. This may be evident on many dimensions: mental, emotional, spiritual. At this high level within the needs hierarchy, the job becomes part of a life plan to achieve fulfillment, enjoyment and even actualization of one's very identity.

Emotional aspects of interactions between people fall into a group of similar, limited categories. Interactions in a supervisory or management context are often "laced" with:

1. *Issues of power*, deriving from one's need to have control and influence over others.
2. *Issues of approval*, deriving from a need for affection, or to be liked;
3. *Issues of inclusion*, deriving from the need to be accepted in a social group;
4. *Issues of justice*, or need to be treated fairly and equitable;
5. *Issues of identity*, deriving from a need for autonomy and self-fulfillment.

The skill of "identifying positive intent" encourages managers to look deeper into what drives particular people in work situations, with the assumption that understanding the intent will provide clues about how to develop a productive communication strategy with this person.

The approach forces you to perform an analysis when you are communicating with others. You need to ask yourself, "What is this individual after? What are the objectives or agendas that help to explain this person's communication and behavior? What needs and priorities drive the person? What does this person seek in interpersonal interactions on the job?"

Managers that identify positive intents in their staff perform an analysis of the fundamental needs that underlie certain workplace communication and behavior. The following are four common intents that managers can assess in an individual under their supervision.

❑ One set of individuals may be highly task-oriented. Their motivation is to **get it done.** This group values eliminating obstacles that interfere with task accomplishment. Individuals of this type cringe at the prospect of participating in inefficient meetings or excessively processing decisions that may result in delays in getting things done. They are anxious to see the final result, and then to move on. When interacting with this type, it is best to keep your communications brief, decisive and to the point.

❑ Another group may be more process oriented. These types focus on **getting it right.** Details <u>and</u> process are now important. Quality is paramount. Errors must be avoided. Deviations from accepted methods not acceptable. Communications between managers and those who are focused on **getting it right** demonstrate the value of planning, step-by-step processes and a shared awareness of time and resource constraints. More extensive communication and decision-making processes are valued if they result in minimizing mistakes.

❑ Another group may place the most value on *getting along*. Here, social needs predominate. Bonding is important for this group. Communications with this type emphasize finding common interests, sharing ideas and emotions and building closeness. Managers flexing to meet the social needs of certain employees find ways to keep the individual from being isolated or involved in solitary assignments. Team-building communication and activities are highly valued. Small talk and good-natured humor is experienced as part of positive human relations between leaders and their staffs. More extensive communication is valued for its role not only in getting it right, but in developing relationships that foster a unified team effort.

❑ A fourth group looks for ways to *get appreciation*. This style is driven by ego, a need to "shine" in the eyes of others. With these types, consistent positive feedback is very useful and motivating. Any criticism of this type needs to be layered between upbeat, positive, reinforcing statements. Rewards, compliments and consistent reminders of "jobs well done" motivate this person. Getting it done, getting it right and getting along are of less importance than getting noticed and appreciated.[4]

Empathic managers will listen for clues about which of these groups best describes the "positive intent" behind an individual's communication and behavior. They will probe intelligently for the larger issues at hand. They will then reinforce this positive intent, at times doing so as part of employing the "sandwich technique" we discussed in Chapter 10 that precedes corrective messages.

Instead of adding fuel to conflicts, this technique eases tensions, adds perspective and creates a bridge to problem resolution. People respond to insightful assessments of their behavior, especially when the ultimate message is supportive and even more so when it is right on target. Employees respect managers who can look more insightfully at the human dimensions of problems. They appreciate the emotional intelligence that this leadership behavior shows.

People Styles

A similar model for understanding how different personalities manifest themselves at work is presented by Drs. Robert and Dorothy Grover Bolton in their book on "People Styles at Work."[5] They advocate that:

- All of us have a dominant style, a "comfort zone" related to how we interact with the rest of the world.
- Each of the four dominant styles comprise about 25% of the population.
- You can't change your dominant style.
- No style is inherently better or worse than another.
- Although people with similar styles obviously share many traits, you are nonetheless also different from others of your style. Put another way, you are far more than your basic style.
- Acceptance of the four essential people styles enables you to work creatively in flexing to different styles.

The Boltons' "People Styles" model, which corresponds highly with other models for teaching conflict management skills, separates people into four essential types shown graphically in Figure 2:

Figure 2: Robert Bolton and Dorothy Grover Bolton's Model of "People Styles"

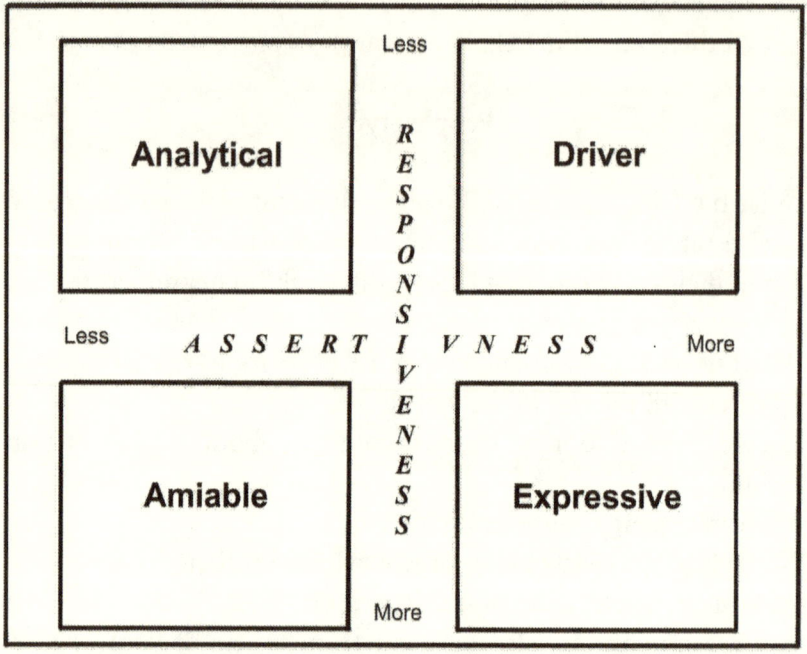

Let's try to understand each of these "People Styles".

➢ *Analyticals*: These individuals combine considerable emotional constraint with less than average assertiveness. Analyticals will tend to be those who are:
   o The most perfectionistic of the styles;
   o Appalled by a "Ready, fire, aim" strategy to making decisions;
   o The "get it right" type—they want to be certain of making the correct choice;
   o Systematic, well-organized and task-oriented;

- o Attracted to data-driven decision-making. The more data, the better;
- o Very prudent in risk-taking;
- o Comfortable with solitary work and personal activities (staying at home rather than going to a party or after-work get-together, reading books, etc.);
- o Loyal when going gets rough;
- o More low-key and quiet; they do not wear their emotions on their sleeve;
- o Likely to lean back in a chair even when making a point;
- o Someone who thinks about what they are saying as they say it, and even interrupt themselves and begin a new thought that came to mind—a trait that often confuses listeners;
- o Favors written over spoken communication;
- o An intellectualizer of feelings;
- o Punctual for appointments but tardy on deadlines

➤ *Amiables:* These individuals get things done in a manner that is less assertive than average, combined with more than average responsiveness. As you can see from Figure 2, the Amiable and the Analytical share a similar level of assertiveness (lower level). Therefore, there will be some similarities between these two styles. The difference between the two styles lies in the degree of responsiveness they each exhibit. The Amiables show considerably more emotion than the Analytical. Amiables will tend to be those who:

- o Are team-players;
- o Prefer working with others on projects, particularly in small groups or with one other partner;
- o Do not seek the spotlight and avoid ego clashes;
- o Find ways to integrate conflicting ideas;
- o Are easygoing and likable;
- o Especially sensitive to other people's feelings;

- o Perform well in service-oriented positions or responsibilities;
- o Value what has been created and strive to preserve it;
- o Comfortable doing routine procedures and following processes established by others.
- o Reluctant to "tell it like it is" for fear of alienating others.

➤ *Expressives:* People in this quadrant combine a high level of assertiveness with much emotional expression. Expressives tend to be:

- o The most outgoing and flamboyant of the styles;
- o Like bright colors, bold statements and eye-catching projects;
- o Thrive in the limelight and gravitate to "center stage";
- o Restless and energetic;
- o Link up with others in everything they do;
- o Have a strong personal network;
- o Dreamers who are bold and imaginative;
- o Impulsive—they act or speak first and think later;
- o Those who prefer to work according to opportunities rather than according to plans;
- o Playful and fun-loving;
- o More into talking than listening;
- o More people-oriented than task-oriented;
- o Someone who speaks to find out what they are thinking;
- o Able to tell it like it is.

➤ *Drivers:* This style blends higher-than-average assertiveness with lower-than-average responsiveness. This People Style is:

- o Very results, bottom-line oriented;
- o Very independent;
- o Very decisive;

- o Able to change mindsets easily;
- o Fast-paced and purposeful;
- o Likely to excel at time management;
- o Factual but not detailed, rational but not theoretical, direct and to the point;
- o Able to bulldoze through an agenda he/she prefers;
- o Task-oriented;
- o Able to have sincere feelings for people, but may not talk about it as much as the "Amiable" and "Expressive" types;

Backup styles

In the context of gaining deeper understandings about the challenges of relating effectively with individuals who present different fundamental styles of behavior, it is also useful to assess how these styles manifest themselves under stress. After all, stressful situations raise the bar in terms of the importance of developing management human relations skills.

The Boltons describe how a *backup style* comes out under extreme stress. The backup style emanates from one's basic style, but it is more extreme due to the powerful effects of stress. The backup style is more evident in conflicted situations at work, especially those between people.

According to the Boltons, the switch from normal to backup behavior is not conscious but rather is automatic. A person's normal style becomes extreme, or "overkill." In a backup style mode:

- o *Expressives,* who are usually socially engaging, *attack.*
- o *Drivers,* who are usually directive, become *autocratic.*
- o *Amiables,* who are typically cooperative and supportive, become *acquiescent.*

o *Analyticals*, who are usually quiet and less emotional, become *avoidant* of participation and emotional involvement.

It is interesting to note that the stress-induced "backup" styles of Expressives and Drivers appear as core elements of several "blind spots" characteristic of impaired executives, which were described by Robert E. Kaplan in his book, "Blind Ambition: How Driven Managers Can Lead Better and Live Better."[6] For example, Kaplan describes a common management blind spot as "Drives Others," which is manifested by:

o Pushing others too hard, and burning them out;
o Micromanaging or taking over instead of delegating;
o Coming across as abrasive or ruthless and insensitive to the emotional harm that this abrasiveness/ruthlessness causes in others.

Another one of Kaplan's blind spots that is relevant to the Driver is labeled "Power Hungry," which is manifested by:

o Seeking power for his or her own interests, rather than the organization's;
o Pushing a personal agenda regardless of other perspectives;
o Being exploitive.

Even more interesting is that Kaplan's other blind spots are aberrations of a "need for appreciation." These blind spots include "Insatiable Need for Recognition," "Blind Ambition," "Need to Seem Perfect" and "Preoccupation with Appearances." All of these leadership problems can be viewed as both normal people styles gone astray because of an inability to manage stress.

"Flexing" Strategies to Different People Styles

The Boltons emphasize that "style flex" is a way of <u>adapting</u> to another person's "process," rather than a way to conform to his or her point of view. "Style flex" is goal-oriented; it is intended to build better rapport and thereby manage conflict.

> "It is about relating constructively while appropriately disclosing your perspective on things as well as listening empathetically to others. The better the interpersonal process, the more likely that people accurately hear each other and creatively resolve conflicting opinions."[5]

"Style flex" is a "temporary adjustment of a few behaviors to improve the results of an interaction."[6] The skill focuses on changing yourself, not changing the other person. The primary leverage you have for improving a relationship, according to the Boltons, is your own behavior.

The Boltons advise a four-step approach that begins with identifying one's own style and the style of the other person. The next step is to plan future interactions based on this identification of styles and flexing suggestions they make. The third step is implementing the plan, and the final step is evaluating the results so that the process can be improved upon.

Here is a grid that summarizes the Boltons suggestions about flexing to the four different people styles (Analyticals, Amiables, Expressives, Drivers):

Table 1: Flexing Recommendations for Amiable Types

Your People Style	Other Person's People Style	Recommended "Flexing" Strategies to This People Style
Amiables	Analyticals	o Be more task-oriented. o Deemphasize feelings. o Be systematic. o Be well-organized, detailed and factual.
	Expressives	o Pick up the pace—move more quickly than usual, speak more rapidly than usual, address problems more quickly than usual, make decisions more quickly. o Demonstrate higher energy. o Focus on the big picture-expressives like to take a "macro" view of things. o Say what you think. o Facilitate self-determination—give expressives freedom, don't be a stickler for rules.
	Drivers	o Pick up the pace. o Demonstrate higher energy. o Be more task-oriented. o Be a bit more formal and businesslike. o Deemphasize feelings. o Be clear about your goals and plans. o Say what you think. o "Cut to the chase"—concentrate on high-priority issues; present main points; "if in doubt, leave it out." o Be well-organized in your communication. o Recommend pragmatic solutions.
	Other Amiables	o May want to temporarily use behaviors of a different style ("Opposites attract/Likes repel") o One of you may need to be more assertive and task-oriented.

Table 2: Flexing Recommendations for *Driver* Types

Your People Style	Other Person's People Style	Recommended "Flexing" Strategies to This People Style

Driver	Expressives	o Make personal contact.
		o Focus more on feelings.
		o Cooperate with Expressive's Conversational Spontaneity.
		o Be open to the Expressive's fun-loving side.
		o Give the Expressive recognition.
		o Communicate on the Expressive's "wavelength."
		  • Expressives like face-to-face or telephonic interchanges, but summaries of the discussion may be needed in writing.
		  • Steer clear of the "nitty-gritty." Don't overdo facts and logic.
		  • Highlight recommendations of others.
		  • Demonstrate concern about the human side.
		  • Provide incentives when possible.
		o Provide considerable freedom.

	Analyticals	o Slow your pace- talk slower, don't rush decisions or force deadlines.
		o Listen more, listen better.
		o Don't come on too strong.
		o Communicate on the Analytical's wavelength:
		  • Be prepared.
		  • Provide detail.
		  • Be accurate.

	Amiables	o Make genuine personal contact. o Slow your pace. o Listen more, listen better. o Focus more on feelings. o Be supportive. o Provide structure. o Demonstrate interest in the human side.
	Other Drivers	o Avoid power struggles. o Be more negotiable. o Listen more and listen better. o Find a temporary way to be less assertive.

Table 3: Flexing Recommendations for *Driver* Types

Your People Style	Other Person's People Style	Recommended "Flexing" Strategies to This People Style
Expressives	Amiables	o Slow your pace. o Listen more, listen better. o Don't come on too strong. o Be supportive.
	Drivers	o Be more task-oriented. o Deemphasize feelings. o Plan your work and work your plan. o Be well-organized with your communication. o Avoid power struggles.
	Analyticals	o Slow your pace. o Listen more, listen better. o Don't come on too strong. o Be more task-oriented. o De-emphasize feelings. o Be systematic. o Be well-organized, detailed and factual.
	Other Expressives	o One of you needs to be more serious and detail-oriented. o Look to add strengths of other styles.

Table 4: Flexing Recommendations for *Driver* Types

Your People Style	Other Person's People Style	Recommended "Flexing" Strategies to This People Style
Analyticals	Drivers	o Pick up the pace. o Demonstrate higher energy. o Don't get bogged down in details and theory. o Say what you think. o Speak in practical, results-oriented terms. o Facilitate self-determination.
	Amiables	o Make genuine personal contact. o Focus more on feelings. o Be supportive. o Provide structure. o Demonstrate interest in the human side. o Don't overdo facts and logic.
	Expressives	o Make personal contact. o Pick up the pace. o Demonstrate higher energy. o Focus more on feelings. o Cooperate with the Expressive's Conversational Spontaneity o Be open to the Expressive's fun-loving side. o Give the Expressive recognition. o Say what you think. o Communicate on the Expressive's wavelength. o Provide considerable freedom.
	Other Analyticals	o Try ways to be more decisive. o Make an effort on the relationship. o Be forgiving with errors.

While these grids include a lot of information and seemingly involve overly-complex decision making in the context of many, simple day-to-day interactions, following the Boltons' model becomes quite intuitive. Style flexing grows to be second nature once a basic understanding of people types is achieved. We promise, you will not need a plastic-wrapped reference sheet or hand-held computer with you at all times in order to make decisions about interacting with others productively. What you will need is a firm grounding in the four people styles and in the other five people skills we have discussed. A willingness to adapt to the people around you is of fundamental importance. It is like the emphasis we placed on being "other-oriented" when we discussed practicing empathy.

Many of us find it hard to adapt, and our resulting defensive position becomes, "I am the way I am, and I don't think I have to change my approach to suit other people." This is a limited and short-sighted view of your relationship-building activities at work. It more or less says, "I don't care about the natural differences between people." It says, "My personality and style is best, and people should change to be like me." Sounds pretty obnoxious, doesn't it? Do you really want to come across like that to others?

Flexing to other people styles means you do care, you do have an interest in reading people, you are emotionally self-aware and you take a more psychologically-minded, emotionally intelligent approach to leadership. Yoga instructors preach, "Flexibility is strength." This is the capstone skill because it unifies all the *SOLID People Management* competencies together into an "other-oriented," adaptable and seasoned leadership style that can take your leadership practice to the highest level.

Coaching Yourself in *SOLID People Management* Competencies

Section Introduction:

Now that you have learned the six essential human relations practices in our leadership skill development model, it is time to practice them. In this Section, we review each of the skills separately, then provide you with some practical exercises that mirror the management coaching process. As we noted earlier, you are able to approach this Section from a self-help perspective if you wish. If this is your preference, we advise you to keep a written log of your reactions, impressions and findings that emanate from performing the skill-building exercises we recommend.

To facilitate keeping this log, we will number sub-sections of this skill-building "manual" so that you can note the corresponding exercise or question to which you are responding. Hopefully, this will make it easier for you to refer back to the exercise and question to which you provided a response.

If you work through this "manual" with a coach or other helping professional, you want to keep a log of your insights anyway, for longer-term future reference. Your coach may add other questions or issues that he or she would like you to address in relations to a specific skill or skill-building exercise. This 1:1 management coaching process can be very dynamic and it is useful to maintain some documentation of all the content stimulated both by the book and by your individual coach.

In the final part of this section, we provide an Internet website where readers can self-administer an appraisal instrument related to your management people skills. You will need to involve others in a 360° appraisal of your human relations skills. You will receive a comprehensive report just as if the appraisal was performed for you by your employer (*see Appendix B*).

12

Practicing Empathy

Skill Review

> o **Empathy is** a critical communication <u>skill</u> that becomes engrained in a people-oriented management <u>style</u>.
> o **The more adept you become at communicating empathetically,** at sensing what others are thinking and feeling, **the better equipped you will become at knowing what messages to send and how to frame them.**
> o The definition of empathy is **"understanding and responding to the unique circumstances of another."**
> o **Empathy is "feeling with"; sympathy is "feeling for."**
> o **Empathic listeners do:** ◆ address what is left unsaid; ◆ set aside their biases and prejudices; ◆ allow the other person to explain his/herself fully; ◆ connect with the other person's emotions without getting too carried away with them ◆ focus on the conversation without distraction.

> o **Empathic listeners do <u>not</u>:** ◆ spend time mentally rehearsing what they are going to say; ◆ tend to rush in and fix things with their "good advice;" ◆ listen to part of what is said and ignore the rest; ◆ make up their minds before they hear the entire scope of what is said; ◆ connect everything the person says to their own experience, not considering the unique circumstances of the other person.
>
> o **Expressing empathy involves:** ◆ asking open-ended questions; ◆ slowing down; ◆ paying attention to your body; ◆ learning from the past; ◆ letting the story unfold; ◆ setting limits.
>
> o **Empathy is very useful in resolving arguments or conflicts. Empathy is evident when you are able to:** ◆ restate the other person's views, to the other person's satisfaction; ◆ seek first to understand, then to be understood.
>
> o **Developmental stages of expressing empathy to another person in an interaction are:** ◆ mimicking back other person's content; ◆ rephrasing the content; ◆ expressing the feeling; ◆ rephrasing the content and expressing the feeling.
>
> o **Other ways of connecting empathically include:** ◆ finding common ground; ◆ blending; ◆ bridging to identification with the feeling.

Self-Assessment of Relative Strengths and Challenges:

Use the following scale to rate yourself on the empathy-enhancing skills listed above.

1. This is a relative strength of mine. I do this frequently and I am comfortable with this skill.
2. This is neither a relative strength nor a relative "development challenge" for me. I occasionally use this skill and get positive results, but

there are also times when I could use the skill to good effect but I do not. There is certainly room from improvement on this skill.

3. This is an aspect of empathy in which I need marked improvement. I do not use this skill, or I use it very rarely, despite the fact that there are times when it would be valuable for me to do so.

* We like this term better than the more pejorative term "weaknesses."

"Practicing Empathy" skill	Self-assessment (1, 2 or 3)
o Are able to "feel with" others around you at work, particularly those who report to you. You make an effort to understand and respond to their unique circumstances.	_____
o When listening to others, you are able to: • Address what is left unsaid............................. • Set aside your biases and prejudices.................... • Allow the other person to explain themselves fully.......... • Connect with the other person's emotions without getting too carried away with them..................... • Focus on the conversation without distraction......... • Avoid mentally rehearsing what you are going to say when the person stops speaking....................... • Avoid "rushing in" to fix things with your "good advice."...................................... • Avoid listening to only part of what is said and ignoring the rest............................. • Avoid making up your mind before you hear the entire scope of what has been said..................... • Avoid connecting everything you hear the other person say to your own experience, rather than considering the unique circumstances that this person .... • Ask open-ended questions to probe for all available information and avoid defensive responses............ • Slow down the pace of conversations when it is important to do so...................................... • Pay attention to your body's reactions to the interaction, and reflect it to the other person as appropriate....................... • Learn from the past and use this experience to gain valuable perspective on current challenges........... • Let the other person's story unfold..................... • Set limits to refocus on here-and-now issues and feelings..........................	_____ _____ _____ _____ _____ _____ _____ _____ _____ _____ _____ _____ _____ _____ _____ _____
o You demonstrate an ability to re-state other person's statements, arguments or issues to their satisfaction before proceeding to making your own statement or arguments, or before identifying your issues. You seek first to understand, then to be understood.......................................	_____

o You **use** some or all of the developmental stages of expressing empathy: mimicking content; rephrasing the content; identifying the feeling; and, rephrasing the content <u>and</u> identifying the feeling.......................................	＿＿
o You look to **find common ground** as way of expressing empathy and resolving conflict.................	＿＿
o You **blend** your experience with those with whom you interact and share how you can **identify** with common experiences and feeling, when it is appropriate to do so and serves to develop more understanding (rather than being self-serving).........................	＿＿

The skills for which you have rated your skill level as 2 and 3 are those on which you should focus your skill improvement efforts. Keep a copy of this self-assessment handy for occasional reminders of the skill challenges you are looking to improve.

The following is a recommended way to *practice your empathy skills* in your work environment. Perform this exercise and make note of (or share with your coach) your experience and reactions to the exercise.

1.0 *Practice Exercises*

Ask a person that reports to you to meet in your office to discuss an update of a project of status of an assignment.

As you begin the meeting, ask an open-ended question of this person. The question can be either unrelated or related to the assignment (your choice). Examples might include:

"(Person's first name), tell me how are you holding up under all the changes we are going through here."
or
"Before we start, let me ask you, what has been the most challenging part of getting this project completed?"

Listen carefully to the person's response. Practice empathy by using the techniques discussed in Chapter 6 and listed above. Try the different developmental stages of expressing empathy—mimic content, rephrase the content, reflect the feeling. Consider things that might be left unsaid. Then, summarize for the other person what he or she has said, and ask for confirmation that your summary is accurate. Continue this interaction until there is mutual understanding.

1.1 Move on to the project that you brought the person in to discuss. Ask as many open-ended questions as you can to gather data and probe for understanding the other person's on the status of the project. Listen empathically—let the explanations, i.e., the "story" unfold. Again, practice the advanced communication skill of *rephrasing the content and reflecting the feeling*. As in Part 1, summarize the key points discussed and the action plan going forward. Gain corroboration from your employee that this summary is accurate and that the plan makes sense.

Exercise Review

In reviewing how you performed in practicing empathy in a workplace interaction, a professional management coach might ask the manager some or all of the following questions:

1.2 How did you establish an environment where you could have an empathic interaction?

1.3 Was it hard for you to listen carefully and non-judgmentally? Explain.

1.4 What technique works for you in clearing your mind and focusing on trying to understand and respond effectively to the other person?

1.5 Were there times when you needed to remain silent or use techniques to allow the "story to unfold?" How do you feel about allowing an interlude of appropriate silence? How do you continue to show your involvement in the dialogue during a silence?

1.6   Did your summaries of what you thought you had heard correspond to what the person was trying to say? What was the worker's reaction when you asked them whether your summary of their viewpoint was on target?

1.7   What did you "read" about the other person during the interaction? What did you share with them about what you were reading in them?

2.0   *Another exercise to practice empathy:*
Reflect back: think of a time when you <u>did not</u> practice empathy, or when you did not act empathetically.

2.1   Why did you choose this incident?

2.2   What was occurring? What was the interaction like?

<u>2.3</u>   **What were you feeling at the time (prior to the interactions)? For example, were you upset about something else, like a marital dispute, child-rearing problem or financial difficulty?**

2.4   How did you react that was less than empathetic?

2.5   What was the outcome? Are there ongoing ramifications?

2.6   What would you have done differently?

3.0   **A final exercise to understand empathy in action:**
In the next week or so, make an effort to observe empathy—or lack of empathy—in action at work. You might observe incidents that you experience directly, such as an exchange between you and your boss, a decision that you were part of that will affect people under your supervision or a general example of caring or non-caring behavior of which you were a part. You might also observe others' interactions at a safe, impartial distance, and analyze how the individuals involved are or are not expressing empathy.

3.1 Explain the observations you made. How did it make you feel?

3.2 What were the results of the parties' practicing or non-practicing of empathy?

3.3 What could have happened differently if empathy had been practiced?

3.4 What is your plan for future interactions of the sort you witnessed?

13

Expanding Self-Awareness

Skill Review:

- Those who make an effort to *expand their self-awareness* do so by:
  - o *Uncovering their blind spots.*
  - o *Hunting for feedback every day.*
  - o *Asking people above, below, across, and outside your organization for input on how you are doing.*
  - o *Taking the pain that sometimes accompanies getting corrective feedback to help secure your power to grow.*
- Expanding one's *emotional self awareness*, through coaching, sensitivity training, counseling or other methods, allows managers to:
  - o Know which emotions they are feeling and why;
  - o Realize the links between their feelings and what they think, do and say;
  - o Recognize how their feelings affect their performance; and
  - o Have a guiding awareness of their values and goals.
- Those invested in the process of understanding themselves and how they are perceived by others are open to:
  - o *Psychological testing*
  - o *360-degree appraisals*

4.0   *Self assessment—Sentence completion exercise:*
An issue that is useful to address as one attempts to gain emotional self awareness involves one's <u>sources of frustration</u>. It is useful and important to uncover one's own role in how circumstances or interactions with people develop into bothersome and frustrating situations. The following sentence completion exercise uses the key aspects of Bennis' formula:

Self-awareness = Self-knowledge = Self-possession = Self-control = Self-expression

Complete these sentences to stimulate self-awareness and personal reflection about important aspects of this formula.

Complete these sentences:

4.1   *Self-awareness*: "I become most easily frustrated when the people around me _____(*your frustration stimuli, a.k.a. your "buttons"*)_____.

4.2   The way I know I am frustrated is that my body _____(your *physical signs*) _____.

4.3   When frustrated at work, my communication with others is usually marked by _____(*how you verbalize frustration*)_____.

4.4   I then tend to _____(*how you act/ behave when frustrated*) _____."

=

4.5   *Self knowledge*: "Hanging on to feelings of frustration is self-defeating for me because _____(*insights into how feelings impact negatively on personal behavior*)_____."

=

4.6 *Self-possession and self-control*: "To move from knowledge to action, I will handle my feelings of frustration with others more effectively if I am able to _____*(how you will exhibit confidence and perspective)*_____."

=

4.7 *Self-expression:* "In situations when I feel frustrated with others, my goal is to have the self-control to say "___*(alternative ways to verbalize frustration)* _____.""

5.0 *Practice Exercise*

Pick an upcoming week when you will be in the office and around your fellow workers all five days, Monday through Friday. During this week, make a special effort to "hunt for feedback every day." Make a conscious and deliberate effort to ask others—subordinates, peers, superiors, human resources staff, other people you come in contact with a great deal, e.g., copy office staff, receptionists, food service workers—for feedback. Ask people in a meeting you led about how useful the meeting was and how they felt about your meeting leadership. Ask those to whom you circulated a memo/email or to whom you issued a report or analysis what their impression was of what you wrote. Be creative in how you frame the feedback-seeking invitation. The input could be as simple and lighthearted as asking someone if they like your shirt-necktie combination, or as significant as asking a customer for feedback about how satisfied they are with your work. Log the feedback for your review at a later time.

Questions a coach might ask:

5.1 Was there a pattern to any of the feedback, or was it rather random?

5.2   How did it feel asking for the input? Were you defensive? Did it get easier to seek feedback the more you did it?

5.3   How do you think the other person or persons responded to you feedback-seeking statements or questions?

5.4   What did you learn about yourself?

5.5   What did you learn about your work performance?

5.6   What did you learn about other people, which you will find useful going forward?

5.7   What immediate changes, if any, are indicated in your behavior or actions?

5.8   What is you longer term plan for continuing to expand your self-awareness?

Another Practice Exercise

6.0   Consider an instance when you lost—even for a brief moment—your self-control at work. What happened? What behavior(s) did you engage in? Anger? Raising your voice? Saying hurtful things that you later regretted? Showing high level of emotion?

Let's review some pertinent questions about your emotional self awareness.

6.1   How adept are you at labeling your emotions? Do you know the difference between different emotions, like feeling anxious versus feeling depressed?

6.2   What type of behavior from others upsets you the most at work? Why do you think that is?

6.3   Before previous instances when you lost self-possession or self-control, did you step back and ask what you were feeing and why? Did you consider how your emotional state going into the interaction affected the outcome of the interaction?

6.4   How impulsive are you? What techniques or emotional self-awareness might "short circuit" your more impulsive actions or expressions?

A Final Exercise

7.0   Observe individuals who have poise, self-possession and self-control, ideally in the work setting but also in the community around you.

7.1   How do they express themselves?

7.2   What verbal techniques do they use?

7.3   What hints do they give out about how emotionally self-aware they are?

7.4   Do they share their self-awareness insights, like "I am not terribly creative, so could you help me develop such-and-such?" thereby modeling how introspective processes takes form in more socially-appropriate, people-engaging behavior?

Log your observations as a reminder of successful behaviors and how they are effected. Look for opportunities to try these successful behaviors in interactions you have with others.

14

Following "Golden Rule" Principles

Skill Review

> o Remain mindful to treat others as you would want to be treated yourself.
> o Regularly turn the tables hypothetically to gain perspective on the emotional impact of statements or decisions you make on those most affected by these actions
> o Be fair and honest.
> o Show respect and tolerance.
> o Embrace diversity.

Self-assessment: how faithfully do you apply Golden Rule principles?

Rate yourself on some of the following basic skills related to being respectful, honest, fair and tolerant. The rating scale will be the same as it was in the _Practicing Empathy_ skill review:

1. This is a relative strength of mine. I do this frequently and I am comfortable with this skill.
2. This is neither a relative strength nor a relative "development challenge" for me. I occasionally use this skill and get positive results, but there are also times when I could use the skill to good effect but I do not. There is certainly room from improvement on this skill.
3. This is an aspect of empathy in which I need marked improvement. I do not use this skill, or I use it very rarely, despite the fact that there are times when it would be valuable for me to do so.

Respectfulness:

Respectful behavior	Self-Rating (1, 2, or 3)
I greet people warmly and remember their name.	___
I listen without interrupting.	___
I use "please" and "thank you" to all levels of staff when making a request or after having a request satisfied.	___
I am prompt for appointments, meetings and commitments. When circumstances occur which cause me to be running late I notify the party expecting me that I will be late and when they can expect me.	___
I apologize promptly to aggrieved parties when I have done something harmful, neglectful or for which I am sorry.	___
I look people in the eye and make good eye contact throughout an interaction.	___
I am never abusive.	___
I keep people informed as appropriate.	___
I acknowledge others' opinions as valuable and consider them when making decisions.	___

Honesty

I do not speak lies or half-truths to avoid the unpleasantness of having to speak the whole truth.	_____
I provide genuine feedback, both positive and negative, to others as a means to others' self-awareness.	_____
I look for opportunities to give genuine positive feedback.	_____
People believe what I say or communicate.	_____

Fairness

I do not "play favorites" or show preference for one person or group of persons over another person or group of persons.	_____
I follow policies, procedures and established guidelines.	_____
I make decisions based on what is right for the team, department or organization rather than what is right for me or for a specific person.	_____
I involve others in decisions to gather different points of view before making these decisions.	_____
I consider the true merits and relative value and experience of people when making personnel decisions.	_____

Tolerance and Diversity

I value opinions that are different from my own.	_____
I value backgrounds that are different than my own.	_____
I avoid sterotypes and biases.	_____
I value cultural differences and how they can contribute useful perspectives to the organization and its mission.	_____

8.0   *Practice Exercise*

For the next two weeks, make a focused, concerted effort to consider "Golden Rule" aspects about any disagreements or frustrations you experience at work. In other words, put yourself in the position of the person with whom you do not see "eye to eye" about some work matter. Try to gather insights about how you would want to be treated if your roles were reversed.

8.1   How difficult did you find it to reverse roles and consider the other person's perspective?

8.2   Is your perception of the disagreement or frustration any different now than before applying "Golden Rule" principles?

8.3   What did you learn about the other person or people associated with the disagreement or frustration? Did you attempt to corroborate this assessment? Example: "If I put myself in your place, I would feel…"

8.4   What did you learn about yourself?

9.0   *Another practice exercise*

Think back to work incidents when "Golden Rule" principles were not applied. People were not treated with respect, honesty, fairness and/or tolerance.

9.1   What was the situation?

9.2   How were you involved?

9.3   What were the ramifications of the incident and associated behaviors?

9.4   How did this situation make you feel?

9.5   If you could relive this incident what might have been different if the party or parties had treated each other as they would like to be treated?

10.0 *A Final Practice Exercise*

In day-to-day work situations, observe how "Golden Rule" principles could be applied. Constantly ask yourself, "Is this how I would want to be treated? Is what I'm saying to this person being conveyed in a way that I'd want a message conveyed to me?"

10.1　Are your decisions or actions different as a result of applying "Golden Rule" principles?

10.2　What impact does this approach have on your self-awareness, self-knowledge and self control? Do you find yourself less impulsive when "Golden Rule" principles are considered? Explain.

15

Maintaining Proper Boundaries / Setting Appropriate Limits

Skill Review

This issue in management human relations is related to **exercising proper judgment** in situations that pose a threat of compromising your leadership authority. This judgment is powered by self-possession and self-control, which emanates from expanding self-awareness.

- Those who are able to maintain proper boundaries and set appropriate limits are able to:
  - Always avoid unambiguous boundary violations, such as romantic relationships at work especially with subordinates, exchanging lewd or culturally insensitive communications, borrowing money from subordinates or taking part in immoral or illegal activities with co-workers.
  - See the difference between work relationships and personal relationships.
  - Apply criteria that asks if the interpersonal behavior has the opportunity to compromise one's leadership role or position of authority to situations requiring judgment about personal closeness at work.
  - Develop and adhere to a personal policy about physical touching/contact at work.
  - Work through new realities of a position of authority with former co-workers, to establish new parameters of the work and personal relationship.
  - Avoid reporting relationships within families, or work these through if necessary on an interim basis.

11.0 *Self-Awareness Exercises for Maintaining Proper Boundaries / Setting Appropriate Limits*

Consider your personal relationships at work.

11.1 To whom do you feel closest on a personal level at work?

11.2 Are there any work relationships that test your willingness to assert your authority when you need to?

11.3 Do these relationships affect the way you interact with the individuals involved?

11.4 Do you act or communicate differently with those to whom you feel closer?

11.5 If you answered "Yes" to any of the final three questions, indicate the following:

The person's position with respect to your position:

- ☐ Superior: person supervises your boss
- ☐ Direct supervisor
- ☐ Peer—Same level of authority as you have
- ☐ Subordinate: reports to you
- ☐ Not a direct report but must interact with them occasionally on organizational matters

11.6 **The nature of the boundary/authority issue with this person:**

- ☐ We are close friends and this friendship transcends our formal working relationship.
- ☐ We used to have a different reporting relationship at work with each other than we do now.
- ☐ Other: _____

11.7 **The consequences of blurred/improper boundaries:**

- ☐ Lax or laxer supervision than you provide to others.
- ☐ Person is given special considerations or information.
- ☐ Occasional indiscreet comments or actions that are "just between the two of you."
- ☐ Other: _____

11.8 Are you ever uncomfortable in performing your role at work given the blurred/improper boundary?

- ☐ Yes ☐ No Explain: _____

_____

11.9 What if anything do you plan to do about the blurred/improper boundary?

_____

12.0 *Practice Exercise*

12.1 Make a list of your subordinates. Rate each 1, 2 or 3, using the following scale. *It is acceptable to use fractions if this fraction would better represent a better rating of your opinion.*

1. I feel close to this person personally. We interact outside work. I enjoy their company both at work and outside work. If one of us left the organization, it is likely we would stay in contact with each other.

2. I feel professionally close but not personally close to this person. We rarely interact outside of work. I do not expect to interact with this person except as it relates to our respective jobs within the same organization. If one of us left the organization, our relationship would end at that point.

3. My relationship with this person is "strictly business." The relationship is neither professionally nor personally close. We never interact outside of work. We can interact within our respective work roles but we would have no reason to interact beyond these work roles.

Name of Subordinate/Direct Report	Rating (1, 2 or 3)
_____	_____
_____	_____
_____	_____
_____	_____
_____	_____

Now consider your management style, decisions, the productivity of these subordinates and instances when you needed to set limits or exercise your authority.

12.2 Are there differences in your comfort level in exercising your authority with subordinates with whom you have different personal relationships?

12.3   For example, are you more lax in your supervision of one person versus another person?

   o   Has this comfort level impacted your managerial actions or decisions?

   o   Is a role clarification indicated with any of your subordinates?

13.0 _Another Exercise_

In your experience, think of an instance when a blurred or improper boundary occurred around you—not to you personally but to someone you worked with, worked for, taught you, etc. This involves an instance when you observed another person developing a personal relationship that transgressed appropriate boundaries.

13.1   What were you and others who also witnessed this behavior thinking about this relationship?

13.2   How did it affect your esteem for them and their reputation with others around you?

13.3   Did the people involved try to keep up a façade that it was a normal working or professional relationship? If so, why didn't this deception work?

13.4   What could you learn for yourself about how they behaved and what the outcome was in this instance?

16

Criticizing Artfully

Skill Review

Criticizing employees' performance can be difficult and uncomfortable, but it is an inevitable aspect of managing others. We know of no manager who has been able to avoid instances when subordinates' errors or poor performance need to be addressed.

---

o   Criticism is "artful" when managers:
  - Build an experienced view of how interpersonal communication can be molded to particular circumstances.
  - Balance the importance of the message being delivered, i.e., that the performance needs improvement, with the importance of delivering it in a way that does not undermine the feedback but rather encourages its acceptance and creates motivation for the desired performance improvement.
  - Resist rash, impulsive, demeaning attacks. An artful approach is thoughtful, not reactive.
  - Expand their personal skills for motivating human behavior beyond highly critical performance appraisal and "shape up or else" ultimatums. They approach opportunities for performance correction with empathy and perspective.
  - Exert self-control and refrain from "shooting from the lip."

---

o   Managers utilize the "sandwich technique," the core aptitude of refined diplomacy and tact. Criticism is communicated by:
  - ALWAYS starting with a positive statement.
  - Layering the "bad news" or criticism after the positive statement.
  - ALWAYS completing the interaction with an affirming statement, ideally that blends the initial positive statement with an expression of confidence that performance will be corrected and things will move forward from this point on.

o   Other techniques include:
  - Get the facts straight.
  - Choose the best timing.
  - Avoid criticizing in public.
  - Control the setting.
  - Condemn the deed, not the doer.
  - Use "you" sparingly.
  - Probe empathically with open-ended questions.
  - Select key issues and restrict yourself to them.

o   More advanced artful criticism techniques include:
  - Don't expect to eliminate defensiveness entirely. Remain calm and firm.
  - Reflect feelings in the interaction.
  - Examine your heart going into the interaction.
  - Defuse anxiety and defensiveness with humor, particularly self-effacing or self-critical humor.

14.0   *Self-Assessment Exercise*

Think of the last instances when you were forced to confront poor performance or a mistake a subordinate made.

14.1   Consider the context…was it in a formal performance review or "in the heat of the moment?"

14.2   Was the timing optimal?

14.3   Did you begin and end the performance criticism with a positive and affirming statement about the person?

14.4   How might your criticism have been more artful?

14.5   Are you comfortable using humor to lighten the anxiety and create rapport?

14.6   In your judgment, which of the points and skills might have been most useful in the actual interactions you have had when a subordinate's performance was criticized?

14.7   Which of these skills are natural for you, and which do you need to develop?

14.8   Did you follow up and remain attentive to opportunities to reinforce desired performance in the period following the meeting when you were critical of a subordinate's work?

15.0   Follow up Exercise:

At work, through media you observe or in other interpersonal interactions you witness, identify instances when an individual uses the Sandwich Technique as a way of artfully criticizing or conveying bad news.

15.1   How did they perform the Sandwich Technique?

15.2   What was the other person's reaction?

15.3   Did you find that this person executed the Technique artfully?

16.0   *Practice Exercise*

Try out the Technique within your family setting. For example, you could use it in a parental role when you need to confront a child's acting out or misbehavior.

Example with younger child: "You've been very well-behaved today. Right now, though, you are out of control. Let's take a little time out so we can get back to that well-behaved little (boy) (girl) I saw earlier."

Example with older child: "Your study habits have been really great this semester. You're doing all your work and getting good grades. But that doesn't mean that you can stay out later than the time when I expect you home. Let's have you stay home tomorrow so we can think about getting back to the responsible behavior you've been showing so much of lately."

16.1   How did you feel using the Technique?

16.2   What was the response like from your child?

At the same time, try out the Sandwich Technique at work whenever appropriate.

16.3   Did the Technique appear to lower the other person's defensiveness?

16.4   Did you have any problem identifying the positive comments to make?

16.5   Did you follow up after the criticism to support positive behavior/work?

16.6   How did the person respond to the follow-up?

17

Flexing To Different People Styles

Skill Review

- Managers skilled in human relations:
  - o Are intrigued by the nature of stylistic differences between individuals.
  - o See a payoff when they nurture more intrinsic rewards for good job performance that are specific to particular types of individuals.
  - o Analyze peoples' interpersonal communication styles as a way to develop a strategy for building relationships with these individuals.
  - o They do so even when these personal styles are quite different from their own.
- "Style flex" means that managers evaluate the people style of co-workers and make temporary, purposeful adjustments to these co-workers natural personality as a way of establishing rapport, building respect and focusing on establishing a productive working relationship.

- Peoples' styles are rather evenly divided into four major groups, based on their relative assertive and responsive behavior. These four types are labeled: Drivers, Expressives, Amiables, and Analyticals.
- Managers need to evaluate their own style then flex to the other person's style accordingly.

17.0 *Practice Exercise*
Identify your own "people style."

17.1 Which "people style" do you believe is yours? Why?

17.2 What other "people style" might apply to you?

17.3 Why is this secondary style less significant for you than your primary "people style"?

17.4 Next, from the group of individuals with whom you work or have worked in the past, identify one representative from each of the "people styles" (the "*Driver*" type, the "*Analytical*" type, the "*Amiable*" type and the "*Expressive*" type) discussed in Chapter 11. These representatives should be rather overt examples of these types, rather than those with who present a blending or combination of the traits.

17.5 Consider the following hypothetical situation: A customer has asked for you to re-do a piece of a recently submitted project in a different way. This requires you to inform a member of your team that was involved in the project that the customer wants a re-work and insists on a short turnaround time frame for getting the re-work accomplished. For different reasons, you expect that each of these discussions may elicit some negativity or contentious reaction.

Remember that the key to "style flex" is that the primary leverage you have in establishing a creative and productive discussion involves your insight about others' people style, and that it is you that must adapt in order to accomplish your immediate goals. Also remember that your style flex is contingent on what "people style" you have identified for yourself.

17.6   How might you begin your interaction with a "Driver"? With an "Amiable"? With an "Expressive"? With an "Analytical"?

17.7   What aspects of each style are important to keep in mind for this interaction?

17.8   Which interaction, or which people style", do you feel will be the easiest for you to "flex" to? What interaction might be the most difficult for you? Why?

17.9   How comfortable are you in flexing your approach to others, rather expecting them to adapt to you?

18.0   *Another practice exercise*

Think about a contentious interaction you have had with another person at work, one that caused you frustration, anger or emotional discomfort.

18.1   What was this other person's "people style?"

18.2   Does the "people style" model help you make sense out of why the disagreement occurred or its negative outcome? Explain.

18.3   Using the "style flex" methods after identifying your people style, how might you have handled this interaction more productively?

19.0   *Flexing to people styles in your personal life*

Consider the "people style" of your spouse, significant other or family member.

19.1   Can disagreements that you have with any of these loved ones be explained by a lack of "style flex" on your part or others?

19.2   In what ways can you adapt to others' people styles to get more out of these relationships?

A Final Thought on the Prospect for Personal Change

A point we made early in this book bears repeating. Often we are asked, "How do you train managers to be, in essence, better people? Doesn't a talent for human relations involve interpersonal skills that need to be well-engrained by the time an individual assumes management responsibilities?" Our answer is "Not necessarily." We find people are motivated both by an interest in self-improvement and by "pain," or the negative consequences—emotionally and from the perspective of a jeopardized career—of not relating well with others. As the saying goes, "No pain, no gain."

Regardless of the catalyst for change, the fact is that "change happens." But it takes work—hard work for people with very little natural aptitude in dealing with other people. This is especially true about the foundation skills we advocate.

To relate well with people, to be a well-respected boss that we'd all love to work for, you need to practice empathy. You must listen actively, get outside yourself and focus on the unique circumstances of other people. You need to uncover your blind spots and build your emotional self-awareness. That way, you will understand other people because you understand yourself. Routinely ask yourself if your decisions are fair, respectful, honest and tolerant, because that is the way you would want decisions made that affect you. Value your position of authority and avoid situations that may undermine this authority. Look for ways to communicate performance feedback, especially when improvement is needed, by motivating instead of tearing down the person. Adapt to others to build rapport. Do these practices because you have an interest in people and in human behavior. You will experience many rewarding human connections as a result. We have seen time and again that a leader's progress toward better human relations does not go unnoticed. People skills matter, and they really are good business!

Appendices

A—Seven step management coaching course

B—Directions for self-administering 360° appraisal on management human relations skills

C—Internet sites for self-administering psychological tests, with professional scoring and report.

Appendix A: <u>A Seven-Step Management Coaching Course</u>

Management coaches do the following:

➜ STEP 1. Share information and build and alliance with client manager.

<u>OBJECTIVE:</u> ◆ Orienting manager to coaching process ◆Defining roles and expectations ◆ Building foundation of trust ◆ Motivating the manager to become engaged in growth process

➜ STEP 2. Assess strengths and weaknesses.

<u>OBJECTIVE:</u> ◆ Compiling results from assessments already performed ◆ Completing own assessment through interview that explores the client manager's educational background, career path, family make-up and issues, goals and objectives—both personal and professional, here-and-now supervisory issues and health status, e.g., level of fitness, ways stress is managed, outstanding health concerns, medications used, alcohol/drug abuse history, including tobacco.

➜ STEP 3. Lay out a formal plan.

<u>OBJECTIVE:</u> ◆ Tailoring and fine-tuning a course of action for manager to follow, with goals, milestones, progress measurement time lines and means to measure progress ◆ Encouraging building self-awareness through soliciting feedback, both on job and in coaching sessions

➜ STEP 4. Guide and direct the manager as he/she implements the plan.

<u>OBJECTIVE:</u> ◆ Supporting client manager as new skills are practiced ◆ Monitoring plan: Are planned actions being performed? Are goals being met within the established time frames? ◆ Role playing challenging situations: allow client manager to practice skills in non-threatening way ◆ Reality testing fears and concerns

163

➡ STEP 5. Reinforce positive results.

OBJECTIVE: ◆ Pointing out evidence of improvement ◆ Pointing out rewards of implementing new skills

➡ STEP 6. At pre-appointed time, perform a broad reassessment.

OBJECTIVE: ◆ Making final refinements to plan ◆ Tapering coaching involvement as self-awareness grows and new skills are incorporated in client manager's practice

➡ STEP 7. Document progress and provide blueprint for self-administered awareness-building and skill development

OBJECTIVE: ◆ Transitioning the client manager to a self-coaching process ◆ Documenting key aspects of coaching and progress made in coaching, for client manager to keep with him/her for occasional review

Managers receiving coaching do the following:

STEP 1. Learn what management coaching is and how it is performed. Develop an openness to outside help.

STEP 2. Participate in testing and interviews aimed at identifying management strengths and weaknesses.

STEP 3. Participate in developing a formal leadership development action plan that:
- utilizes existing assessment data,
- includes personal goals and
- establishes time frames for completion of agreed-to tasks.

STEP 4. Solicit guidance and direction from management coach in implementing the plan. Perform exercises and practice skills suggested in the plan. Share skill development experiences with coach. Monitor self-awareness, sharing new understandings about "inner life", such as one's feelings/emotions.

STEP 5. Accept positive reinforcement when given. Consolidate gains and begin building these gains into management practice.

STEP 6. Reflect on progress made and its meaning for the future. Become more self-reliant for seeking feedback within personal sphere (peers, subordinates, bosses, customers).

STEP 7. Summarize progress made on plan developed in Step 3. Keep coaches' progress report accessible as point of reference for use in ongoing self-awareness process.

Appendix B

To self-administer an Internet-based 360° appraisal of the skills *SOLID People Management* competencies outlined in this book, please visit our website:

www.workandpeople.com.

Click on the link for "Perform a Multi-Rater Assessment of *SOLID People Management* Competencies."

This link describes the method for conducting your own 360° multi-rater appraisal of each of the six essential human relations practices we describe in this book. It includes the cost, method for payment, sample e-mail messages asking individuals to rate you using our instrument and a description of the report you will receive once all your raters have completed their evaluations.

You may email us with questions or comments at
bookcomments@workandpeople.com.

Appendix C

Internet Sites to Self-Administer Recommended Psychological Tests

Come to **www.workandpeople.com** and click on "Self-Administer Psychological Tests." Here you will learn about psychologist-run sites that are partnered with Work & People Solutions. Also, you will be able to click right through and self-administer the tests we recommend in Chapter 7. You may pay with a credit card and receive an online report of findings from licensed psychologists. Work & People Solutions has pre-screened these psychological testing vendors, and we use these Internet sites regularly with our own clientele.

Notes

Chapter 1

1. Motto used by Ernst & Young, LLP. In "Message from Our Chairman," Jim Turley writes, "Our vision and strategy are twofold: first, it's to be known in the marketplace as the firm where people want to be, because it's the firm that <u>puts people first</u>...." See <u>http://www.ey.com/global/Content.nsf/US/Careers - Student - Message from our Chairman</u>.

2. Motto used by the Hay Group to describe company's approach to consulting services and to developing firm's own talent. See <u>www.haygroup.com</u>.

3. Carole Sansone, Editor, "Intrinsic and Extrinsic Motivation: The Search for Optimal Motivation and Performance," Academic Press, August, 2000.

4. Douglas McGregor, "The Human Side of Enterprise: 25th Anniversary Printing," Irwin/McGraw-Hill, 1985.

5. From review of McGregor's theories published on Internet website <u>http://www.accel-team.com/human_relations/hrels_03_mcgregor.html</u>

6. *Ibid., from* Internet website:
   http://www.accel-team.com/human_relations/hrels_03_mcgregor.html

7. Ron Willingham, "The People Principle. A Revolutionary Redefinition of Leadership," St. Martin's Griffin, New York, 1997.

8. *Ibid.,* Introduction.

9. *Ibid.,* p. 12.

10. Abraham Maslow, "Maslow on Management," John Wiley & Sons, New York, 1998: Chapter on "Further Notes on the Relationship Between Psychological Health and Characteristics of Superior Managers (Notes from Likert)," pp. 94-101.

11. *Ibid.*

Chapter 6

1. Eric Maisal Ph.D., "*20 Communication Tips at Work*", New World Library, 2001: Tip #17, "Practicing Empathy".

2. *Ibid.*

3. Arthur Ciarmicoli, Ed.D., Arthur P. and Katherine Ketcham, Ph.D., "*The Power of Empathy*", A Plume Book, Published by The Penguin Group, 2000.

4. Covey, Stephen R., "*The 7 Habits of Highly Effective People*", A Fireside Book, Published by Simon & Schuster, 1989: p. 240.

5. Maisel, *op.cit.*

6. Rogers, Carl, "On Becoming a Person: A Therapist's View of Psychotherapy", Houghton Mifflin, 1961.

7. Covey, *op. cit.*

8. *Ibid.*, p. 241.

9. Ciarmicoli and Kecham, *op cit.*

10. Covey, *op. cit.*, pp. 248-249.

Chapter 7

1. Warren Blank, "*The 108 Skills of Natural Born Leaders*", AMACOM, New York, 2001: p. 33.

2. *Ibid.*, p. 34.

3. Warren Bennis, "*On Becoming a Leader*", Perseus Books, Cambridge, MA, 1989. The formula presented in this chapter is located in the Chapter entitled, "Knowing Yourself."

4. Daniel Goleman, "Working with Emotional Intelligence", Bantam Books, New York, 1998.

5. *Ibid.*, p. 54.

6. *Ibid.*, p. 69.

7. *Ibid.*, p. 54

8. *Ibid.*

9. *Ibid.*, p. 68.

10. Blank, *op. cit.*, p. 53-54.

11. *Ibid.*

12. For a useful, brief historical overview of how Dr. Kurt Lewin pioneered the use of T-groups to advance organizational human relations, go to Internet website:
www.soi.org/orgchange/growth&development.html

13. Blank, *op. cit.*, p. 53.

14. *Ibid.*

15. This description of the MBTI® is taken extensively from the explanation of this psychological test and Jungian theory provided on Internet website www.itd.net.

16. The California Psychological Inventory™ is authored by Arthur G. Gough, PH.D. and published by Consulting Psychologists Press, Palo Alto, CA.

17. The description of the CPI™ is based on information located at the website www.cpp-db.com.

18. For descriptions of the Thomas Killman Conflict Mode Instrument and the FIRO-B™, see www.feedbackshop.com.

Chapter 8

1. Janet Gallant, "*Simple Courtesies—How To Be a Kind Person in a Rude World*," Reader's Digest, Pleasantville, NY, 1998.

2. Robert Bolton and Dorothy Grover Bolton, "*People Styles at Work*," AMACOM, New York, 1996: p. 111.

3. *Ibid.*, p. 111-112.

Chapter 9

1. Jack Welch, "*Straight From the Gut,*" Warner Books, New York: 2001. Chapter 13.

Chapter 10

1. Goleman, *op. cit.*, p. 263.

2. Some leadership development authors advocate shying away from use of the word "criticism" as it implies blaming and other negative emotional behaviors. We use criticism to convey any behavior that seeks to correct performance flaws, even when undertaken in a very positive, affirming manner.

3. Sachs, Randi Toler, *"Productive Performance Appraisals"*, Amacom, New York, 1992.

4. See the following resources for excellent reviews of these techniques and the Advanced Artful Criticism techniques starting on page 117: Armstrong, Michael, *"Performance Management—Key Strategies and Practical Guidelines, 2nd"*, Kogan Page, London, UK, 2000, and Deep, Sam and Sussman, Lyle, *"Smart Moves For People In Charge"*, Perseus Books, Cambridge, MA, 1995.

Chapter 11

1. Willingham, *op. cit.*, p. 138.

2. Rick Brinkman and Rick Kirschner, "*Dealing With People You Can't Stand*," McGraw Hill, Inc., New York, 1994: p. 50.

3. Abraham Maslow, "*Motivation and Personality*," Harper Books, New York, 1954.

4. Robert Bolton and Dorothy Grover Bolton, *op. cit.*, Chapter 2.

5. The remainder of the chapter focuses on presenting the model outlined in Robert Bolton and Dorothy Grover Bolton's highly useful and practical book, "*People Styles at Work*," *op. cit.*

6. Robert E. Kaplan, "*Beyond Ambition: How Driven Managers Can Lead Better and Live Better*," Jossey-Bass, San Francisco, 1991.

About the Authors

Stephen E. Kohn is a highly experienced management coach who has provided leadership development services to executives for over 15 years and employee counseling services and organizational development services for over 20 years. Formerly Executive Vice-President of Paul Sherman and Associates, Mr. Kohn is now President of Work and People Solutions, a human resources management consulting firm. He specializes in helping organizations address troublesome people problems and helping managers develop interpersonal human relations skills. Mr. Kohn earned his undergraduate degree from Cornell University and his graduate degree from Adelphi University.

Vincent D. O'Connell is a consultant in human resources and behavioral sciences. He currently serves as Principal and Senior Partner at Work & People Solutions. Previously, Mr. O'Connell worked in consulting positions with the Hay Group and Buck Consultants. He is a graduate of Brown University and attended the Baruch College/Cornell Joint Program in Industrial Labor Relations, concentrating in human resources management. He has published articles on behavioral health benefit topics in several professional journals, including *Compensation and Benefits Management*. He has led many corporate workshops in management communications skills, both oral and written.